THE EPIPHANIES PROJECT

Twenty Personal Revelations

PETER AVILDSEN   NATALIE MARIE BROBIN

JEANNE FOOT   TIMOTHY GAGER

BLAINE GRAY   LISA HARRIS   JOHN FERREIRA

AMY LIZ HARRISON   CHRIS JOSEPH

JEFF KOBER   BARBARA LEGERE   HEIDI LE

HEATHER LEVIN   SARA ONEIL

SAMANTHA PERKINS   KOREY POLLARD

ERIN RANTA   BETH ROBINSON

SUELEN ROMANI   SUSAN ZINN

Manifest Books

ISBN: 978-1-7376646-1-1 ebook

ISBN: 978-1-7376646-0-4 paperback

Although this publication is designed to provide accurate information in regard to the subject matter covered, the publisher(s) and the author(s) assume no responsibility for errors, inaccuracies, omissions, or any other inconsistencies herein. In certain cases, incidents, characters and timelines have been changed for dramatic purposes. Some names and identifying details have been changed to protect the privacy of individuals.

Book design by Sheila Smallwood.

Cover art by Catherine Just.

CONTENTS

FOREWORD

Everything is execution.

That's what I said to Chris Joseph when he told me he'd had an important epiphany in the middle of the night, which had been followed by another: that he wanted to partner with another writer, Beth Robinson, on editing a collection of essays about epiphanies.

I knew my response was annoying.

I mean, it's one thing when someone's not excited about your epiphany, but when they're also not excited about your new book idea? Double annoying.

But I see far too many people wandering this earth talking about their brilliant ideas and far too few executing them. Brilliance is rare, as is motivation, and executing an idea brilliantly is even rarer. It's far easier to talk about a great idea than it is to do anything with it.

I've concluded that ideas are meaningless. I mean, the book every woman I know loves—*Eat Pray Love*—is about a woman going on a trip. If Elizabeth Gilbert had told me she'd had the epiphany that she needed to write a book about going on vacation, I would have been equally unenthused.

I'm humbled to report that almost a year after my exchange

with Chris, he handed over the book he co-curated with Beth that I most definitely hadn't encouraged them to do. And I'm humbled because it's been executed in that rarest of rare ways: brilliantly.

It's also a bit of a heartbreak. There are essays in here about losing a child to suicide; about rape; about killing; about alcoholism and trauma and abuse and 9/11. As a reader, you'll be put into the shoes of a soldier in combat, a young woman being shamed after a sexual assault, a man losing his siblings, a child being abused by a mother and much more.

And yet there's so much hope. There are epiphanies about love that manage to be profound, epiphanies about divorce that manage to be hopeful, epiphanies about racism and dysfunctional relationships and codependence and kindness that manage to be authentic and unique. How do you feel when the father of a boy you've killed in an accident tells you how much your kindness meant to his son? How do you feel when your drug-addicted son begs you for permission to take his own life? I've never read any collection that places the reader more in the not-always-comfortable shoes of its contributors.

For me, this is especially surreal, since this is a book made up of the work of people who only met because of a writing group I started near the beginning of the 2020 stay-at-home order. Feeling powerless, I'd announced to my newsletter subscribers and social media followers that I was going to be writing for an hour every day on Zoom, and anyone who wanted could join me. I saw it as a life raft, something to cling to in a time of uncertainty.

Not expecting anyone to show, I offered bribes: free access to my courses for anyone who came and asked me a writing or publishing question. But I quickly realized that bribes weren't necessary, and that this gathering was as much about connecting as it was about writing.

Together, this group of strangers collected at 10 am Pacific time, their Zoom eyes meeting one another's as they talked about their fear, their uncertainty, their writer's block, their careers, their relationships. Suddenly, this wasn't a group hanging to a life raft, but an actual buoy made up of strangers who were quickly becoming friends. I decided to turn it into a membership program, put someone on my team in charge and give it a name. The Launch Pad Inner Circle was born.

I'm not going to lie—when I learned that members were flying to visit one another and joining each other's pandemic pods, I started to feel a little left out. Similarly, as other people kept signing up for the group, I worried about the new kids in town; surely they'd feel left out of this tight-knit community of people who'd never sat in the same room together. But, one by one, I'd watch the new person become a regular contributor to the group and for everything to coalesce again.

I wasn't doing anything to make this happen. The buoy just kept growing. And as it grew, Chris and Beth—who had both shown up that first day—continued to ask people to contribute to this anthology. In the end, they gathered 20 essays, all from members of the Inner Circle.

This would be meaningful enough, but my job in this foreword is to talk about the writing. Now, in addition to being an idea snob, I'm also a writing snob. When someone says, "Everyone tells me I'm a great writer," I will often think but not say, "That's great. Do you go up to a doctor and tell them that everyone tells you that you're a great surgeon?" Writing is just one of those things that everyone thinks they can do, and there's no one there to tell them they can't since judgment about writing is subjective.

The one thing we all agree on is that great writers have one thing in common: they write. Regularly. Perhaps at 10 am, with a group of strangers-turned-friends, every weekday. In doing that over the past year, the contributors to this book became spectacular writers before my eyes. They didn't take classes or go get MFAs. They didn't read every book out there about writing. But they wrote every day, and in doing that, they transitioned from people who write into writers.

The proof is in these pages.

These stories provide alternately powerful, tragic and sweet exposure to the pain and beauty of life. But they gave me something more: the long-overdue epiphany that a book about epiphanies is a brilliant idea.

—Anna David, May 2021

INTRODUCTION

One day about six months ago, Chris Joseph, a member of my daily writing group, reached out to me with an idea.

He told me that upon finishing writing his (very good) book, he realized he'd left out a story. It was about an epiphany he had one night during his cancer journey. It occurred to him that lots of writers in our group probably had stories of realizations that changed their lives, and he wanted to know if I was interested in helping him compile a collection of these stories.

I was.

We hammered out all the prosaic stuff—the who, what, when and how of it. And then we reached out to the writers whose work you will see in this collection. They all wrote great stories, but then there was editing and rewrites and more rewrites—and as we were collecting all the finished pieces, we realized we needed an introduction to the book.

I told Chris the introduction should be about his epiphany about creating the book, and Chris being Chris, he said, "It shouldn't be about me."

"No, it's not about you," I replied. "It's the story of this book."

So, since he wouldn't write it, I did—both to give credit

where it's due, and to let you know that this collection of epiphanies is based on an epiphany that woke Chris Joseph out of his sleep, one that inspired him to inspire me to help gather these wonderful, personal and wildly disparate stories from friends in our writing group, and to turn them into a book.

If you would like to get to know our friends a little better, their bios are in the back, many of them including websites and social media accounts and links to their work. I know I'm biased, but I think you'll want to get to know them all.

—Beth Robinson, co-curator (with Chris Joseph) of this book

ACCEPTANCE

BARBARA LEGERE

"Ms. Legere, I'm afraid that if I let Keven out of custody, he won't make it long enough for a county-funded bed to open for him. The level of heroin in his system was alarming. If your son's drug use continues at this level, chances are he will die."

This warning came from a judge who had called me up to the bench to speak in private.

My son, Keven, discovered heroin at age 17 when a friend begged him to try it. Others in the room warned against it, but he gave in to the pretty girl with a syringe. It was the beginning of 13 years of addiction to heroin. The effects of it allowed him to cope with his depression, anxiety, and paranoid thoughts. Meanwhile, each day, I woke wondering if he was dead or alive and if he'd make it through another 24 hours. At night, every siren, every ring of the phone, made my heart pound in fear.

For the first few years, I was angry. It seemed like he wasn't trying hard enough. I'd stay up all night waiting for him to come home then go to work in the morning. Keven and I lived with my mother and my sister, Therese, and the three of us raised him with unconditional love. Now we had to hide our jewelry, credit cards, and cash, but he still found and sold a lot of our belongings. Occasionally I'd wake up and discover a group of "friends" in his room or sleeping in our garage. It was an endless cycle of rehabs, jail, fresh starts, and relapses.

My goal became to understand not "why is he using?" but "why can't he stop?" Research taught me a lot, but the real insight came from Keven himself. Sitting on the side of my bed late one night, my handsome boy looked at me with black smears on his face. He'd wiped away tears with his heroin-stained fingers.

"Mom, I hate this, but I can't stop," he said. "I swear to God, I really want to quit." I sat up and rubbed his back as he went on. "It's like I feel normal when I'm high. After I use it feels like everything in my life is fine, like I can manage. If I don't use, I just want to die because I hate myself and my life. Plus, I hate what it's doing to you, Grandma, and Therese."

Empathy replaced anger, but my worry and stress were still in full force. I was rarely getting a good night's sleep, so I coped by eating comfort foods and put on 40 extra pounds. My stress level soared, and our codependent connection led me to think that it was my job to rescue my son.

My co-workers noticed I was no longer my cheery, positive self and questioned me.

"I'm trying to take care of myself, but I'm always nervous and stressed," I would reply. I was always on alert for the next traumatic event—arrests, suicide attempts, overdoses, emotional breakdowns, hospitalizations, psychotic breaks. The dark world of drugs kept clawing at Keven, leaving emotional, mental, and physical scars. Peace ceased to exist.

At one point, Keven was at risk of losing his leg because of a dangerous infection he'd gotten from shooting up with dirty needles. I cried in relief when the surgeon told me he'd saved it, but the threat of losing a limb hadn't slowed Keven down.

Then there was another phone call informing me Keven had been on life support for three days, listed as a John Doe after being left for dead in an alley. There was the time they took him in a straitjacket to a mental hospital. Those episodes became common. Every time I felt like I couldn't handle another crisis, I'd come face-to-face with a new one.

The few friends who weren't avoiding me at this point sounded distant when I started talking about Kev, but I had nothing else to talk about. I was fired from a job I'd had for 17 years. Once an excellent employee, I'd become a liability. My mind was no longer focused on my job. This cemented the belief that I had become a failure in most areas of my life—as a mother, as a friend, as an employee.

People remarked how strong I was for being able to handle it all, but couldn't they see I wasn't handling it? The chaos and trauma were taking a toll on me, mentally and physically. After losing my job, I recognized I was in trouble and had lost control of my life. I took the advice that had been offered by everyone, from professionals to strangers, and went to Al-Anon. I found a group just for parents. The idea was to take care of yourself and not let the addict control your life. That sounded like what I needed.

There was one man in the group who lectured us. He believed tough love was the only answer. Half the group agreed. The tough love parents had removed their children from the home and sometimes from their lives. A few bragged about how long they had gone without talking to their child, as if it were a badge of honor.

I'd kicked Keven out several times over the years, and he'd always found other addicts to stay with. They had gotten high together, committed crimes, and endangered their health. I could understand and support the families that had no choice but to remove their child from home, but it went against my maternal instincts. If my son was going to lose his life to drugs, I wanted to have as much time as possible with him while he was still alive.

The Al-Anon group didn't believe in harm reduction, either. I supported giving substance abusers clean syringes and access to

Narcan. Keven already had hepatitis C from sharing needles and his HIV tests had come back both negative and positive. The danger Keven faced was infected abscesses from shooting up in his muscles because his veins were completely "shot out." He was going to use heroin no matter what. At least I could help him be safe in that one way.

My group judged me for enabling him, and in a way they were right. I was enabling him to keep using despite my belief that I was keeping him safe; but I was also enabling him to hear daily that he was not his addiction, that he was a valuable and loveable human being.

Keven was tall, well-built, and covered from head to toe in tattoos. He was the guy girls would call late at night to rescue them from a bad situation on a date or at a party. If a friend liked something he owned, he usually gave it to them. Kev was known for his giggle, which didn't fit with his tough-guy image.

Those of us who knew him were aware of his sensitive soul and his suffering. A psychiatric assessment revealed that Keven loathed himself; he felt unworthy. Turning my back on him would only exacerbate his low opinion of himself. The idea of letting a heroin user hit bottom is dangerous because their bottom is often death. I had to do both: help him and help myself. After two years, I stopped going to Al-Anon. Defending my unpopular views was only adding to my daily exhaustion.

One afternoon, I encountered a young man outside a fast-food restaurant. His name was Daniel, and he held a small cardboard sign that said: *"Hungry, anything helps, God bless you."* I smiled at him and reached into my purse to give him a couple of bucks. He smiled back in appreciation. My fingers fumbled through my wallet; I had no cash.

"Hey, can I buy you lunch?" I asked him instead.

Our conversation over the meal began with ease as he shared a bit about himself, his battle with drugs, and living on the streets. Then he asked about me. As always, I answered by sharing about Keven and what a heartbreaking journey I was on as his mom.

"I feel like I'm grieving my son even though he's still living," I said. Tears welled in my eyes as I uttered those words.

Daniel listened intently and seemed to care about my distress.

"You know the Serenity Prayer, right?" He asked in his kind voice. "It's the acceptance part of it you need to focus on. When you're stressed out all the time and worrying about losing your son, you're fighting against something instead of accepting it. How is that helping you or Keven?" Of course, I already knew this—or did I?

"You know you can let go and love at the same time, right?" Daniel said, smiling with empathy. I sat back and contemplated his words for a moment before the conversation drifted again. Later, I thanked him for his insight, and we parted with a hug.

That evening I sat down to process what Daniel had shared. The Serenity Prayer was a mantra of mine: "God, grant me the serenity to accept the things I cannot change, courage to change the things I can, and wisdom to know the difference." I had accepted that Keven had many debilitating challenges, so what more was there to accept?

The truth engulfed me like a waterfall: I had not accepted that I could not fix or save him. On the surface this was obvious, but deep down inside, most of my angst could be traced to my nonstop quest to *save my son*. Not just help him, but save him. The thought of losing him panicked me, and although I believed Keven had to do the work to save himself, my actions told another story. I wanted sobriety for him far more than he wanted it for himself.

For years I had been offering solutions: rehab, sober living, medically-assisted treatment, and a few unorthodox methods as well. I'd fought his war, losing one battle at a time. Accepting that I could not save him meant I could stop fighting. I could focus on loving Keven as he was instead of trying to fix him, to save him. Could I give myself permission to wave the white flag?

When and if he was ever ready, I believed he would find his way. And while I watched from the sidelines, I could let go of my endless efforts to save him and accept life as it was. Doing so became my steepest mountain to climb—and there had already been plenty of them. Choosing to let go of saving my son put me on constant guard against my old ways of thinking and forced me to make choices based on my own needs. It wasn't easy. I tried and failed and tried again.

The decision to change slowly shifted my life. Rather than feeling constantly pressured, I gradually worried less and smiled more. It seemed like I could take deeper breaths. My attitude became more positive and grateful, and fresh energy filled my being. Yoga and meditation became an enormous help, physically and mentally. I slept better and started to lose the extra weight, embracing a level of self-care that hadn't been a part of my life for many years. Though Keven's drug use continued and I still worried, my life was getting back on track.

In one tender conversation, Kev said he noticed I was less stressed, which allowed him to relax and enjoy our time together with less guilt. His deepest regret was all the distress he'd brought into my life.

"Mom, my friends tell me they can't believe how much you understand about what we go through," he told me one day. "They think I'm lucky to have you as a mom. I tell them I know. It makes me feel proud of you. I just wish you'd stop singing in the car when we're giving my friends a ride." I laughed. His words meant a lot. I enjoyed his drug friends, the only friends who would hang out with him. They were all different and all the same. I became close to several of them over the years and they're all gone now; six of them overdosed and one was murdered.

Keven and I treasured the good days when he wasn't dope sick or too high to function. We laughed, talked, and watched movies and crime shows. We argued politics and pursued our favorite pastimes together. There were also moments where he was so depressed that he'd lie next to me on my bed, hug our dog, and cry as I rubbed his back.

As time went on, I watched as my boy became more despondent. The smiles were less frequent. He existed only inside a black cloud. My heart ached. My love for Keven was deep and never-ending. If only love was enough.

Four months before his 30th birthday, Keven shot and killed himself in his bedroom. The sudden blast reverberated through the house and through my body. I knew what had happened as I ran upstairs to find him. The horror of seeing your child with a bullet hole in his head is unspeakable. I had mentally prepared myself for it for years, but nothing could have prepared me emotionally. All the same, I was grateful it had happened at home, and that I was there with his body as his spirit passed over.

Earlier that morning, we'd talked about how hopeless he felt, and he'd told me, as he did every day, how much he loved me. He allowed me to hug him—a rare occurrence—and I memorized the feel of his arms around me, his cool skin, his broad shoulder where I laid my head. That hug was his special gift to me, a moment I will forever cherish and recall often.

The worst possible thing that could happen had happened. I wasn't angry with Keven for leaving me; I understood he felt too tormented and exhausted to keep going and he sincerely believed I'd be better off without him; of course, nothing could've been further from the truth.

I have a gaping hole in my heart, and some days, the emptiness consumes me. Grief doesn't end. It has a life of its own, surprising me daily with its ups and downs. I laugh at wonderful memories, and I often sense Keven's presence near me. I've accepted this unwanted change as my new phase of life, and I will keep moving forward until the day Keven and I meet again.

Until then, I choose to keep my son's story alive and help others by sharing our mistakes and successes.

Today, I'm often reminded of a quote from *Man's Search for Meaning* by Viktor Frankl, a book Keven read whenever he was in jail or prison: "When we can no longer change a situation, we are challenged to change ourselves."

JONESY AND MOUNT ST. HELENS

LISA HARRIS

Jonesy was my least favorite—cranky and controlling, complete with a shrill screeching cackle that only enhanced my sense of persecution on my weekly treks to her apartment in the South End. But how I wish I had made it to her apartment as scheduled on that rainy afternoon.

Jonesy was one of several clients of mine from UpJohn Chore Services, an agency that deployed young teens like me to help poor senior citizens on fixed incomes with household chores like cleaning and errands. Jonesy's real name was Mrs. Jones, but she insisted that everyone call her Jonesy. It was irritating.

Of the three elderly people I saw on a weekly basis, Jonesy worked me the hardest. She regarded me as her personal servant and acted like I was getting paid thousands of dollars. In truth, she got me for free through a social service program supplied by the county that paid me $3.10 per hour.

Part of why the job was so hard was that it was depressing. The people I worked for seemed to have no family and no friends, and often their homes were in tough neighborhoods and in bad condition. By contrast, Jonesy had a very nice apartment and seemed to have a lot of friends (who were always calling), but she had no appreciation for any of it—only complaints and entitlement. She would compile long lists of tasks she expected me to complete during the two hours I was scheduled to work for her. As she stood over me squealing orders, I worked fast, but I could never quite finish everything despite my best efforts. It made her very angry and meant I was subject to more berating.

On one Tuesday afternoon, it was pouring down rain and I was due at her place at 4 pm. I took my regular school bus to my neighborhood and stopped at Barry's—a local restaurant where I used to work—to get a coffee before boarding the city bus that would take me to her apartment. I was not dressed for the rain, and I was not dressed to clean. I wore black velvet pants and a black velvet jacket over a white frilly blouse. Spiked tan heels completed the ensemble. Somehow it worked.

I clicked up the slick, front steps and entered the restaurant, where I spotted Mark Smith sitting alone with a drink. He was not quite handsome, but certainly not homely either: dark hair, slight build, a mustache and goatee, perhaps 5'10". He wasn't my type—I was nearly 5'11", long and lean, but it wasn't his height that I found unappealing. It was the slightness of his build. I felt like I was bigger than him and for that reason, I was not attracted.

I knew him from the neighborhood. We had met a few times over the past year. He had been engaged to the eldest daughter of one of the most beloved Irish Catholic families at my church. They met in AA, a still relatively unknown group at that time. Word was that she had just broken off their engagement after learning that at age 25, Mark had already spent time in prison, was a former heroin addict and had lied to her about a previous marriage. It was a scandal that rocked our tight-knit community.

I saw him sitting alone at Barry's and I felt sorry for him. He spotted me and asked me to join him. Flattered that a grown man wanted my company, I sat down at his table.

Mark looked sad. A glass of clear liquid sat in front of him, and I could smell that it was booze. I knew he wasn't supposed to drink. I pitied him.

"Would you like a drink?" he asked.

"They won't let me drink here, they know I'm underage," I said apologetically. I was 17 years old, and because I used to work at the restaurant, the staff knew I was still in high school.

"Well then, could we go somewhere and have a drink? I really don't want to be alone today," he said. He looked straight at me. I could see his need.

"I have to go to work soon," I said, thinking of Jonesy.

"That's fine, I'll drop you there. Let's just have a quick drink first."

The prospect of a ride to Jonesy's apartment—instead of the long hike on the city bus in the rain—was appealing. And it felt grown-up to be asked to "have a drink." I had heard of a place that supposedly served underaged kids. We climbed into his Volkswagen Rabbit to make the short drive. Upon arriving, I ordered a glass of white wine and wasn't carded. I knew within minutes that I would not be making it to Jonesy's. I found a payphone and called to let her know.

"How can you do this to me?" she shrieked into the phone. "I need you! What am I going to do?" I told her again that I couldn't make it and that I would come next week. She was furious but I hung up and returned to the table. We drank more. Before I knew it, I was too drunk to walk, and Mark half-carried me out to the car.

❦

I woke up 25 miles outside of Seattle in an abandoned apartment. I could hear Billy Joel's "It's Still Rock and Roll to Me" playing somewhere. I was frightened but too drunk to do anything about it. Mark was on top of me. I was in trouble.

"Please, get off me. I want to go home. Please take me home." My voice sounded small.

But he didn't get off me. And he didn't take me home. Sometime later, I was back in his car. I edged myself as far over as I could. He asked where I lived. I told him. He dropped me without a word.

I immediately went upstairs to my room and changed out of the black velvet pants and jacket. I bunched them up and put them on the floor in the far corner of my closet. I never wore them again. I got in the shower. I replayed the tape, trying to make it come out differently: I left the bar after one drink. Mark dropped me at Jonesy's and though a little buzzed, I managed to clean.

Or: I left Mark at the restaurant. Never got in his car. I sat with him for a moment, long enough to say hello, then went to the bus stop to go to Jonesy's.

Or: I saw Mark as I walked into the restaurant, but having heard all the terrible things about him, I knew better than to stop. I merely waved hello and kept going.

Again and again, I played these alternative scenarios in my head, somehow thinking that if I played them enough, one of them would become the truth. But I couldn't rid myself of the images of what had actually happened: Mark on top of me, the abandoned apartment, the cold sound of Billy Joel singing.

I dried off, dressed and went downstairs. As I sat at the table with my younger brothers, sister and my dad, I knew none of them had any idea about what my life was. I was a straight-A student who had an after-school job. That's what they knew. As we ate, the conversation was about the eruption of Mount St. Helens. An entire family had been killed and so had an old man with lots of cats—16, to be precise. My sister worried about the cats. My dad raged about the irresponsible parents who had taken their two children to the mountain.

Tears welled in his eyes. The family had been discovered in their car, suffocated from the ash. When Mount St. Helens first erupted, I'd seen the plume from hundreds of miles away while riding the bus down I-5. It looked beautiful and extraordinary. In the ensuing days, the ash went east and missed Seattle entirely. I had no concept of the devastation it unleashed. My problems seemed bigger to me.

☙❧

"Yo, Lisa?" It was my ex-boyfriend, Jim, on the phone. It had been four days since Mark had dropped me at my house. I had broken up with Jim some weeks before, and he had taken it hard. Although Jim and I had been together for nearly a year, we had not had sex. I was relatively inexperienced when I met him, and we had planned on waiting.

"Yeah?" I said into the phone, confused as to why he was calling.

"Did you see Mark the other day?" he demanded.

"What?" I asked. My mind began to focus. *How did he know?*

"Did you get in a car with him?" he asked. He was interrogating me.

"Huh?" I fumbled around, mind racing, heart pacing. I knew this was trouble. He didn't wait for a more meaningful reply; he just kept going.

"Did you fuck him? 'Cause he's telling everybody that you did."

☙❧

"You're a lying piece of shit." It was the next day, the day after Jim called, and I stood before my father. "You broke my heart today." He was crying.

Jim had gone to my dad and told him about Mark and what he'd done. Jim urged him to press some kind of charges against

Mark. After all, Mark was a 25-year-old ex-con and former heroin addict. Jim probably had a point: Statutory rape? Getting a minor drunk? But seemingly no one pressed charges about that kind of thing back then. Though I was mad at Jim for telling my dad, underneath, I think I wanted him to. I think I wanted my dad to protect me. Even though I knew the whole thing was my fault, some part of me understood that I was in over my head. I needed someone to stand up for me and take him to task. But that was not to be.

"You broke my heart," he said again. And when my dad's heart broke, he knew only one thing: attack. The pain was too much. And so there we were, predator and prey. As I stood before him while he raged at me with tears in his eyes, I knew that I had hurt him. The damage was done, and it was irrevocable.

The incident with Mark was my fault, I understood this; after all, I had gone with him to the bar. I had been flattered that he asked me. I had enjoyed the attention. It was my fundamental character flaw that caused the whole mess. It had been a trick, a test; the gods were seeing what I was made of, and I had been caught. I had been exposed for my unforgivable vanity, and hence, the gods had struck me down.

In failing the test, I had failed my father. I was not the daughter he thought I was. And as I stood there, I knew there was nothing I could do to unwind the damage. He decreed that I was now on restriction: except for work, I was not to leave the house. And then I was dismissed.

I retreated upstairs. I was alone. God had turned his back on me, my father had washed his hands of me, and I was a pariah—I had fucked the ex-fiancé of the eldest daughter of the most important family in the community. And now, I was nothing.

Many years later, after my father had passed, I was able to put together the last pieces of the puzzle that were scattered on the table that day. By then, I had certainly encountered a therapist or two who had explained to me that the event was not my fault. While it was easy enough to say, it had taken years to absorb that truth, though I had managed it.

Still, despite urgings from members of the many tribes I inhabited over time, I had never been angry with my father. I didn't know why. Then one day, on a walk in the cemetery where he was buried, I told my stepmother about what happened. She'd married my father some years after the incident and didn't know anything about it. But she knew my father. She sat for a moment and then said simply, "Well, he had to blame you. If your dad had truly taken in what had happened, he would have had to kill Mark. And surely he would have." In that shining moment, I was finally able to put words to what I think I had always known: my father had been fighting for his survival, too.

And so it goes for today, as the memories of UpJohn Chore Services and rainy bus rides to the South End continue to fade, I can think of Jonesy and her piercing commands with amusement, and even a little fondness. Perhaps, in the end, that's what we're all doing: trying to survive.

FRANKIE

JEFF KOBER

This is the moment that lives in memory: standing on the brakes, the slew of tires against wet pavement, the thump of the unavoidable contact, the sudden silence. The Bronco juddering to a stop, its engine dead. The vacuum wiper wheezing one final time across the windshield. The boy, his Halloween mask suddenly gone, sliding on his back, his green corduroy jacket, one arm flung out as if trying to hold the moment before. Slipping endlessly away on the rain-slick road, a slow spin through the headlight beams then disappearing in the darkness beyond. The suddenly lifeless form of what had been, just a moment before, a boy.

❦

When I was a sophomore in high school, I didn't have a car. I had a small dirt bike, a Bridgestone 100. Sometimes I'd ride it to school, or I'd drive the Bronco, slow and loud and muddy, that we used for irrigating and checking cattle. Other times, I took the bus. Walk to the end of the lane, a half-mile or so, over the ditch, under the freeway, and wait next to the old highway for it to come.

The first week of school, I'm too old for the bus now, so I'm trying to be *in* the bus but not *of* the bus. I hear commotion a few rows back and turn to see some boys giving a younger boy shit. Never seen any of them before. Three on one. They were grabbing his books, slapping the back of his head. The bus driver was worthless, ignored anything and everything as long as there was no blood or broken bones. The kid was stoic, just trying to ride it out. I got up from my seat and walked back, slapped one of them on his crew-cut head, took a book from another and handed it back to the boy, then picked the other one up by the front of his coat and carried him to the back of the bus where they'd been sitting before, and deposited him in his seat, making sure the others followed. And if I ever see you messing with that boy again, you're gonna wish you hadn't. Okay? I was a big guy, a football player. They listened.

I went back down the aisle, stopped to ask the boy if he was okay.

"Yeah. I'm okay."

"Mind if I sit down?"

"Um, sure. Yeah." He moves his books to give me room.

"So, do you know those kids? Who were giving you a hard time?"

He half turns to have a look at them. "Nah. They're just..."

"Little boneheads?" I offer.

That makes him laugh. "Yeah, they just don't know how to behave. That's all."

"Oh... Simple as that?"

"That's what my dad says." He straightens up a little to imitate his father. "You know, kiddo. Some kids just don't know how to behave."

"Huh."

"They don't have anyone to show them what's right and wrong. So they'll do what's wrong without even knowing they're doing it." He stops quoting. "That's what he says."

"He sounds pretty smart. Your dad."

"Yeah. He is. A *lot* smarter than me."

"You've got quite a few books there. Looks like you might be pretty smart, too."

"Yeah. I am. For a little kid."

"Well. Good."

⚜

We became friends. On days I rode the bus, I'd sit with Frankie. I'd ask him if the other kids were leaving him alone, which apparently they were. After a while, we got into the challenges of school, and math. I did flashcards with him, learning his pluses and minuses. I told him about playing football and riding motorcycles, and he told me about crop rotation—"alfalfa follows corn, 'cause corn eats everything in the soil"—and learning how to snare a prairie dog by laying a little loop of string around the hole of their mound and lying in wait, as quiet as you can be, till one of them pokes his head up far enough to be snared.

I'd never had a friend so much younger than me, but it made sense. Like we were meant to know each other.

⚜

About a week after his funeral, my mother told me to dress up. We're going to see the boy's parents. We are, I asked? Yes. Come on. Get dressed. Your father's waiting for us. I sat in the back of the car as we drove the three or four miles to their farm, just past the feedlot and off the old highway toward the river. I didn't ask what we were going to do, or say, what we might expect, how do we do this. I didn't know how. No one offered conversation. It was silence from the minute we left straight through to our arrival.

We parked in the gravel of the farmyard, dogs barking, then quieting as we got out of the car. Mr. Walston came to the door. He smiled, welcomed us, brought us inside. Said his wife was in the back of the house, in the bedroom, and offered Mom and

Dad a cup of coffee. Mom asked could she go back, and sure, of course you can. Just down the hall there. He walked with her to the hallway. Honey? Mrs. Kober's coming back. That okay? He listened, then nodded to my mother, said go on back. He poured coffee for himself and my dad, handed me a glass of water, and we were invited into the living room. I sat on the couch, Dad on an old wingback chair with doilies on the arms. Frankie's dad sat across the coffee table from me in a chair he'd carried in with him from the kitchen. Atop the mantle behind and above him were framed baby pictures of two boys, Frankie and his brother Jessie, and another of Frankie and his dad dressed in nice clothes. They both were smiling, proud of each other.

"That your boy?" asked my father, nodding.

Mr. Walston looked around and nodded himself. "Yeah. There's our boys." He turned back to us and smiled, sad but genuine. I watched the two of them, awed by the back and forth of the men, seeing the grace of this father who had lost so much so recently and watching my father navigate the unknown of these moments. It was as if they knew some moral code I wasn't yet privy to that directed their conversation. You could hear the boundaries of it as they discussed the price of cattle and sugar, what the new feedlot meant to the valley, how the market looked for next year. Common ground.

There was a wail of grief from the back of the house, a keening of bottomless despair beyond anything I'd ever heard. Beyond the cry I'd heard on the night of the accident, no less fresh but filled now with the weight of every day every day every day my boy is gone, my boy is gone. My breath caught in my throat and I looked away, trying to crawl inside myself so as not to hear. The men dropped their eyes to their hands, to the floor, waiting for the wave of it to subside, and as it did, it became a soft sobbing, and we could hear my mother's voice comforting her, one mother to another.

Mr. Walston raised his eyes, took a breath and began telling us stories about Frankie. How smart he was. How full of life. He wanted to know about everything, followed his father around like the sun rose and set on him, when clearly it was the other way around. He taught Frankie about internal combustion engines as they overhauled a tractor, about crops and cattle, about catching prairie dogs with a string lasso.

"He told me about his new friend on the bus. Came home one day and said there was this older boy who'd protected him from some bullies, and then later, how they were becoming friends. About how special it was to have that kind of friend. How excited he was on the days you got on the bus. He'd watch out the window when they got to your stop, and some days you were there and he knew it was gonna be a good day."

Is he talking about me? And with that thought, the weight that had been pressing me down fell away, and my gaze lifted up and into his eyes and the wholly unexpected warmth there. The idea of Frankie talking about me, and his father sharing it with me now came at me from the side, skirting the black machinery of guilt in my head, making one small mark of compassion and light in the darkness of everything, a gift from this man who somehow didn't hate me.

"Thank you," he said to me. "Thank you for being my boy's friend. It meant the world to him." As if it were just the two of us. As if my father, my mother, his wife, his grief-stricken home, all had faded away leaving him free to offer me what he could, and by looking into my young eyes, having the chance to say goodbye to his own boy in a way that he hadn't been able to do on his own.

I never did lay eyes on Frankie's mother. She stayed back where my mother had joined her, in her own bedroom, or clutching the bedspread in the bedroom of her dead son. Mr. Walston showed us to the door, shaking my mother's hand and thanking her for spending time with his wife, shaking my father's hand and telling him to take care, and shaking my hand and telling me, "You take care of yourself, okay?" And then, again, "Okay?" waiting until I was able to look him in the eye one final time and nod my head. "Okay," he said, and squeezed my hand again before letting go.

Though it took years for me even to begin to know how to take care of myself, I never gave up looking for the way forward. Maybe because of the promise I made to this man because he insisted; I let him be a father to me, and I let myself be a son, for just that moment, to him.

VISION > FEAR

HEIDI LE

T*here is a gun in the...no, I won't do that.*

But what if I just didn't wake up tomorrow?

What if I didn't have to be here anymore?

This particular Tuesday or Friday, or whatever the hell day it was, resembled all the rest. I was lying on the couch with my unwashed hair pulled out of my face—a half-hearted attempt to pull the evidence of my apathy out of my awareness. Sunlight streamed through a slit in the drawn curtains, reminding me that just outside my den of misery, people were flitting about their productive lives.

The warmth and optimism of the sunny day were clouded over by shame, shame that despite living in a nice home with a wonderful husband, I didn't feel "happy"; shame that despite being a songwriter and performer, I wasn't writing, or creating, or singing; shame that I was wasting my time and my gifts; shame that despite having a personal and transformative relationship with God, I wasn't experiencing joy, or peace, or purpose; shame that I couldn't pull myself out of this dark place; shame that everything felt so heavy and oppressive —everything.

Every mundane task seemed to require an extortionate amount of physical, mental, and emotional energy—energy I simply did not possess.

Ugh. I should shower today.

And my hair is disgusting.

And I should cook something for dinner. Anything.

I should do ALL of those things?! What am I, a f***ing triathlete?

Okay, I'm showering, but I can't wash my hair. And I guess I'll order pizza again.

I hate myself.

As though trying to draw water from an empty well, my internal shaming and should-ing voices kept scraping at the parched foundation of my soul. There was clearly nothing left to give. The voices scraped and scraped until they tore through the layer of numbness that covered me and a new kind of pain pierced through the fog of apathy, shame, and depression. It was the pain of staying stuck, and it was immediately unbearable.

Fear of remaining in this stagnant place prodded me to move. I reached for my iPhone, knowing that the solution to this pain of staying stuck was waiting for me just inside the home screen. For months, I'd had "Carolyn Adkins - counselor" safely tucked away in my contacts, patiently waiting for the day when I would feel miserable enough to want to try something new. This particular Tuesday or Friday or whatever-the-hell-day was that day.

My phone felt heavier than usual. It always seemed absurdly ginormous, enshrouded in a poofy, 3D Hello Kitty case. Just below the pink bow on her ear, she was adorably accessorized with nerdy, thick-framed glasses. Hello Kitty looked smart in those glasses, and I sensed an imperceptible knowing nod from her that we should indeed make the call to this "Carolyn Adkins - counselor." *Are you gaining weight?* I silently asked Kitty. We both knew I was stalling. It was the fear of change that felt heavy and scary.

Riiiinnnng...

I felt my chest tighten.

Riiiiiinnng...

Maybe she won't pick up.

"Hello!" Carolyn's cheerful voice floated through the speaker, interrupting the battle between hope and self-sabotage that raged in my mind.

"Um, yes...I'd like to make an appointment," I stammered. "I got your name from a friend and, um, I need your help."

Within a week, I was sitting in Carolyn's office pouring out my sadness, frustration, and shame. The safe space of her presence gave me the freedom to empty the broken parts of my life out into the light. The fears and feelings I had been hiding in the dark didn't seem so scary with the light of compassion shining on them.

I began to see that all the broken parts of my life were really just puzzle pieces—perfectionism, people-pleasing, controlling, excessive caretaking, and a lack of boundaries that left me frighteningly vulnerable. Carolyn helped me label all of the pieces before giving me a priceless gift. She showed me the picture on the front of the puzzle box: codependency. Codependency was the glue that held all the pieces together; codependency was the common denominator.

I learned that this box of dysfunctional puzzle pieces had been created within my alcoholic home and given to me as a parting gift when I moved out at the age of 17. My behaviors were all rooted in fear, and my coping mechanisms worked brilliantly within the ecosystem of an alcoholic home, but they were no longer working in my adult life. Fear had helped me to survive, but didn't I want more out of life than survival?

After a few sessions, Carolyn suggested that I attend Co-Dependents Anonymous meetings and read some literature on the topic. I was all in! I faithfully attended 12-step meetings and devoured any book she suggested on codependency. I was oddly thrilled to have this new label about myself and my crazymaking puzzle pieces. Soon I found myself unashamedly declaring:

"Perfectionism isn't a noble standard in my life, it's codependent!"

"Abandoning myself to focus entirely on others isn't love, it's codependent!"

"Hello, I'm Heidi, and I'm codependent!"

The label didn't feel negative or punitive. It kicked the door to freedom wide open. *After all*, I thought, *it's only when a sickness is diagnosed that a cure can be administered; it's only when a problem has been clearly identified that a solution can be found.*

I felt sick with problems, and I wanted a cure. I was ready for a solution, and suddenly my eyes opened to see it rising up all around me. The authors of my recovery books wrote about how they, too, had once felt sick and stuck. In meetings, I heard my new friends talk about how addiction, codependency, depression, anxiety, and other soul-crushing issues had stolen years of their lives and bankrupted their relationships. They went on to describe how they were healing and were now living lives of freedom, joy, and service.

As they talked about their everyday experiences, I was amazed at how they were able to handle even messy, complicated issues in their lives and relationships. In all the same areas I was clumsily getting tripped up, consistently making matters worse, and generally creating fuel for the ongoing dumpster fire of my personal and professional life, these magical recovery wizards were responding with supernatural wisdom and grace.

Whenever I tried to be "emotionally honest," in reality, I was just vomiting my feelings onto others. The recovery wizards had the wisdom to kindly speak their truth and then let go of the results.

When I first began learning about boundaries, I launched into a full-throttle, boundary-smackdown vendetta in nearly every relationship. In my immaturity, I was just using "boundaries" to try to change and control people. The recovery wizards had learned how to set and maintain healthy boundaries in non-punitive ways.

I could see myself in the messiness of their stories. And, in their healing, I saw a vision for what was possible in my life.

I realized if I wanted to take hold of the peace and freedom that my friends and mentors were experiencing, I would have to be willing to do the work that they had done. If I wanted to experience something new, something better, then I would need to humble myself and embrace the reality that I was a beginner, a clumsy toddler in the realm of healthy thinking and relating. Inspired by my new recovery heroes, I decided I would choose willingness and humility as my daily attitudes to the best of my human ability. And then I kept showing up.

Then, on another ordinary Tuesday or Friday or whatever

heavenly day it was, I realized: *This is actually working.* I looked around at the landscape of my life and relationships to find that everything was being recreated and renewed. The vision of a new life of freedom, peace, and joy had been pulling me forward, little by little, into a better version of myself.

Vision had become greater than fear.

Fear had served me well throughout my life before recovery. Fear motivated me to create coping mechanisms that helped me feel safe for a while. The fear of staying stuck in my familiar misery demanded I make that first call to my counselor, and the fear of relapsing back into the soul-sickness of my raging, untreated codependency made me willing to say "yes" to the unfamiliar process of transformation. It was okay to be grateful for how fear both protected me and motivated me to become willing to change. I could honor the role fear played in my life, knowing it was the best resource I had at the time, and it had served me well.

But vision! Oh, yes! With all the wisdom and clarity of mind that recovery brings, I could look back on my healing journey and see a million ways that God had dropped glimpses of His vision for me into my awareness. While fear served to push me into anxiety-based action, the vision ahead of me magnetically pulled me forward into a better life and a higher calling. While fear shrieked, "You better act! You better move! DO something!" vision gently wooed me forward with glimpses of its beauty and goodness.

I remembered how Carolyn would say things like, "In a year, if you keep doing this work, you'll look back and you won't even recognize this woman who's so worried about what other people think." It was a glimpse of goodness, a vision of my future self, confidently living my own life.

When I came across these Promises of AA in *The Big Book,* they gave me a glimpse of the goodness to come:

We will not regret the past nor wish to shut the door on it.

We will comprehend the word serenity and we will know peace.

No matter how far down the scale we have gone, we will see how our experience can benefit others.

We will intuitively know how to handle situations which used to baffle us.

We will suddenly realize that God is doing for us what we could not do for ourselves.

What an incredible vision for my future!

When I saw my friends navigating life and relationships in ways that I admired and could only hope to emulate someday, those were glimpses of goodness—a vision that empowered me to see myself someday living a life of integrity, emotional honesty, and relational peace.

So, I pressed forward, ineptly attempting to mirror the new ways of thinking and relating that were being modeled for me; I began stepping into these glimpses of my higher self. The process was awkward and painfully slow, but it was working to bring my vision into reality.

One day, as I sat down with my journal, I prayed that God would show me His vision for the remaining scattered components of my life. I'd been writing songs throughout my recovery experience, but I didn't know what to do with them. The desire to "make it" in music had melted away; I no longer wanted to get signed or go on tour. I no longer needed to find my identity in that role, and I no longer wanted to spend my evenings playing music in crowded clubs at a volume that would drown out 12 jet engines running concurrently with 43 KISS concerts. I no longer had a self-created vision for my life, so I asked God for His vision for the gifts and talents He had entrusted me with. Then, I sat quietly and listened.

He answered.

A rush of words flowed to and through me. I poured them into my journal, scribbling frantically in the hopes of recording every bit of the supernatural download I was receiving. I lost myself completely, utterly enraptured by the conversation I was having with the creator of the universe—the creator of my universe. When the flow stopped and I ran out of words to scribble, I felt like I had given birth. I was exhausted and there was a new creation laid out in front of me. It was a vision of goodness I never could have imagined or crafted for myself, even though it all seemed so obvious there in black and white.

The music I had been writing over the past few years captured the raw experiences of my recovery journey—the grief and depression as well as the hope and healing. Lyrics such as these, from a song called "Shelter Me," distilled hard-earned wisdom into anthems of freedom and songs of surrender:

You know the tears come when I lay down to sleep

You know all my fears, they chase me, chase me every day

You hold me near in the shadow of your wings

You hear the prayers I lay down at your feet

You shelter me

These songs didn't just tell my story. They told the stories of so many of us who have felt stuck and hopeless for far too long. They held promises of hope and invitations to freedom.

I realized I had more than just songs to offer and that the

details of this transformational experience needed to be told, honored, and shared for the benefit of others. Out of this revelation, a book and companion album of five soulful, bluesy, rock tunes were born, an outpouring of creativity that tells my story of recovery and redemption.

Since their release, I've performed the songs and shared my story at drug and alcohol treatment centers, recovery meetings, churches, on podcasts, addiction summits, and at the House of Blues. The real privilege of these experiences is the opportunity to connect with hurting people who hear my story and feel safe to say, "Me too. You've put words to my pain; you've shown me the picture on the front of my puzzle box." What an honor to be a light bearer, to show them that the broken pieces they've hidden in the dark aren't nearly as scary with the light of compassion shining on them.

Life in recovery has taught me that I have the power to open my heart and mind to my highest vision for my life. I have the freedom to ask God to show me His dreams and plans for me, and He will always be faithful to meet me in a unique and personal way. And whenever fear makes my path appear dark, I can remember this truth: vision is greater than fear, and I only need a glimpse of goodness to light my way.

LIMINAL SPACE

SUSAN ZINN

I t was a Tuesday morning, like any other morning. I was going a hundred miles per hour, carrying too many Starbucks coffees to my office and listening to a dozen urgent messages from our London headquarters. I caught a glimpse of my reflection in the elevator. *Why did I have that third cocktail last night?* I thought to myself as I felt a headache coming on.

I reached down and adjusted my shoe. I noticed a blister forming on the back of my heel from the four-inch stilettos I had worn the night before to a nightclub opening in SoHo. As I entered my office, I made my rounds, placing the coffees on my friends' desks. They flashed me smiles and mouthed "thank you" as they stayed glued to their calls. As I scavenged my desk drawer, searching for a Band-Aid and Advil, everything and everyone suddenly stopped. It felt like someone had hit the pause button on a digital recorder, freezing me in motion as a boom vibrated through the office.

"What the hell was that?" I asked no one in particular. Still holding my coffee, I walked to the window. Before I took my first sip, a frantic barrage of ringing began. The volume grew steadily louder as phones rang in every direction.

"I just heard a plane hit the North Tower of the World Trade

Center. It's all over the news," my co-worker yelled across the office.

"What? Who do we know that works in the North Tower?" I asked my friends as I began scrolling through my phone directory. My phone rang.

"Hello?" I said.

"Where are you? Are you close to Wall Street?" I recognized my brother's voice immediately.

"No, I am at the office."

"Seriously, Suz, what is going on?"

"I don't know. Everyone is reporting all sorts of information, but I don't know anything specific yet. My office is chaotic. What are they reporting in China?" I asked.

"You don't want to know. It is terrible. People are flipping out."

"This sounds bad. I'm going to call Arthur to see if he is reporting for Channel One News right now," I said. "I hope he can give me more information."

"Call me back as soon as you can, okay? And Suz? Be careful. I love you," he said.

"I love you too." As I hung up the phone, my eyes welled with tears.

I tried to call Arthur and a few friends who worked on Wall Street, but my calls went straight to voicemail. Just as quickly as the ringing erupted in my office, it stopped. No landlines or cell phones were ringing; there were no dings from email notifications. Panic soon began to find its way into the corners of my mind as my colleagues and I frantically tried calling loved ones to let them know we were safe. There was only silence on the other end.

I wanted to see for myself what had happened. Fearing a power outage would follow the cell tower disruptions, I avoided the elevators. I followed the herd of people walking up the 38 floors to the building's rooftop. Unbeknownst to me, thousands of others were desperately trying to evacuate the Twin Towers.

At first, I thought it was an airline tragedy, but conspiracies soon began to swirl around the roof deck. A few people had seen BBC footage, which speculated about something way more sinister. I watched the massive flames and smoke engulf the skyline, wondering: *where is the plane?*

At 9:02 am, I watched in silence as the second plane, United Airlines Flight 175, carrying 56 passengers, flew straight into the south face of the South Tower.

"Oh, my God, what is happening?" I cried. It seemed clear this was not a tragic airline miscalculation. I struggled to identify an emotion far greater than disbelief. I was witnessing the unfathomable. The iconic New York City skyline was gone.

I sat frozen in fear, with a steady stream of tears rolling down my face. Trembling in a thin cotton T-shirt, I could not take my eyes away from my view of the horizon until after the first tower began to collapse in a roaring silence and a tremendous gray-white poof. The second tower soon followed at 10:28 am. *Please, God, I hope everyone got out alive*, I prayed. But I knew my prayers would not be answered.

"I just heard there are more targets," I overheard a man say to a group of people standing close by me on the rooftop.

As people began speculating about more attacks in New York City, I wanted to get off that high-rise building as fast as possible. I descended to find smoke filling the silent streets. The only sounds were an occasional battery-operated radio crackling in the background, broadcasting the news, and sirens everywhere.

I took a deep breath before orienting myself to where I was going. The city's entry points were closed and subways were suspended, so I walked to my apartment on Rivington Street on the Lower East Side, a few miles away from the World Trade Center's destruction. I walked for what felt like hours, aimlessly making my way as I passed hundreds of people going in the opposite direction. We were all covered in the same film of gray dust containing the last remnants of the New York skyline.

As I passed people, I caught their gazes, cementing a knowing of what we both had just witnessed. I spoke to several strangers along the way, asking if they needed help. Some looked like they were in shock. Some had minor injuries. A woman wearing a navy business suit who appeared to be about my mother's age stopped me and asked, "Why are you walking in the wrong direction?"

"I am going home," I answered.

She gave me a perplexed look that said: *Are you sure you want to go there?*

As I entered my neighborhood, I noticed an older woman with a thick accent sitting outside her apartment.

"Sweetheart, do you know what is going on?" she asked. I knelt in front of her in my filthy black designer pants with my mascara-smudged face, and I started to cry. Wordlessly, I hugged her in her pink floral housecoat, her thick body making it hard for me to embrace her completely. I smelled grandmotherly rose perfume. I realized at that moment, at 26 years old, every rule I had followed to live my life now felt meaningless and no longer applied. Nothing was to be trusted in this new dimension, including myself.

⚮

The word *liminality* is often used in anthropology to describe the middle stage of a rite of passage. It is the space in which we have left behind who we once were but have not yet become something else. In the hours that followed the Towers' collapse, I entered my liminal space. I lost my youth with its velvet ropes, late-night parties and designer labels and found myself in the in-between, unsure of who I was to become. I only knew I couldn't go back to who I had been just hours before.

I was in a state of shock when my boss demanded I attend a meeting in Detroit in person the following morning. On September 13th, the day LaGuardia Airport reopened, I boarded a flight. As I entered a nearly empty plane accompanied by US air marshals, the feeling of danger kicked in. I felt every muscle tense as I began scanning the airplane, looking for people who looked suspicious.

I held my breath for the entire two-hour-and-five-minute flight, gripping my armrest and waiting in anticipation for terrorists to overtake the plane. The trip proved to be more than unproductive. The automotive executives I was sent to see only wanted to talk about Tuesday morning. They were talking about it like it was an episode of "CSI" and not something I had just lived through, speculating whether Detroit might be the next terrorist target. I left the meeting bubbling with rage.

Hours later, I arrived back at the Detroit Metropolitan Wayne County Airport seething and angry at the automotive executives' lack of empathy. I was angry at my boss for insisting I travel on a plane a day after witnessing a terrorist attack. I wanted to scream! How could he be so careless? I knew it was a memory that would stay with me for the rest of my life.

I vomited up my fear and rage in the nearest garbage can after passing through the security checkpoint going to my terminal gate. As I sat on the flight back to New York, I started to reflect that sometimes it takes a life-changing crisis to remind us of what truly matters. It was clear that my job wasn't it anymore.

In the weeks that followed, I felt utterly disconnected. Most of my friends had slept through the terrorist attacks. It seemed like everyone I knew, including my friends who lived in New York City, wanted to hear firsthand what it was like to witness New York's downtown streets on the morning of September 11th. I was so grateful for their concerned calls and emails. However, it also made me relive the story repeatedly.

I was alone in my sobriety as I responded to 9/11 emails by cutting and pasting a duplicated message over and over again. People kept asking questions, not realizing their impact. Their questions were sometimes insensitive. Had I seen anyone jump?

Questions like these traumatized me. The flight to Detroit had compounded my trauma, and I knew I was in trouble after leaving my phone in a taxi for the second time in a week.

Like many downtown New York apartments, mine filled up with friends whose apartments were destroyed in the blast, and they brought their animals with them. Soon my apartment housed my friend's black Labrador retriever puppy and Yorkshire terrier, along with my cat, Minca. Steady 24-hour news channels were center stage. We ate pizza almost every night since there was only two-day-old Chinese take-out, two-percent milk, coffee, a bottle of champagne, and little else in my refrigerator. The boxes remained stacked on the counters as reminders.

People came and went, sleeping and lounging on every surface, safe behind the protection of an Army tank parked outside. With their low-hanging rifles, the National Guard stood just yards away on streets near my apartment building's entrance, prohibiting anyone except the residents from going any further downtown. It seemed to me I was on the most exclusive VIP list in the city, but it was the first list I wish I had not made.

I no longer worried about what to wear and what time we were going out at night, nor could I connect with my friends and roommate, who were taking a different route. They were laughing, giggling, and late-night drinking in my living room almost every day to avoid, I assumed, their feelings. I am not sure, really. Maybe they just wanted to feel alive. Whatever it was, I found nothing funny about it.

It felt like I was living in a horror movie, one I didn't want to see but was forced to sit through with my eyes closed, wishing it would end soon. I was no longer having the time of my life and felt like a prisoner in my own apartment. Post-traumatic stress was twisting its way into my body's crevices, making me struggle to breathe at night. It would invite itself into my room, where I had duct-taped fluttering garbage bags over my windows to keep out the ash and death. Like the city, I began to meet my soul in the stillness and it felt like an awakening. I could no longer go back to the life I once lived. The emptiness of that life was now buried in the rubble of Ground Zero.

My refuge during this time was my fire station. It was referred to as "Fort Pitt," Engine 15, Ladder Company 18. I wanted to do something to help. I began making daily stops to offer fresh cookies and lunch—any excuse to be close to the heroes of 9/11. I felt so much shame about how selfishly I had been living my life compared to the first responders. They set off to experience dirt, death and toxic poisons in "the Pile" of Ground Zero every day. What difference was I making in my life?

Yet, somehow, they still shared life, returning to the station where I witnessed a kind of humanity I so longed for in my own life. There was talk of families, there were celebrations of wins over those many months, and there was gratitude. Oh, there was so much gratitude. These brave firefighters were still able to find a moment, a glimmer, a spark, to remind themselves that life was worth living.

It was here that I felt the calling of service, directing my life down a different path. The firefighters at Ladder Company 18 allowed me to experience what it means to have a purpose in life, giving me a direction where I needed to go—a becoming on the other side of my liminal space. My connection to Fort Pitt soon allowed me to stop holding my breath in fear. I began to sleep at night, not worrying that I would not wake up in the morning, and I felt safe again.

My bedside clock read 2:02 am when my cell phone rang.

"Hello, is this Susan?"

"Yes, it is," I replied.

"This is Diane, a nurse practitioner at St. Vincent Hospital. I am calling because you are the sexual assault advocate on call tonight. There is a young woman in our emergency room waiting for you. Can you be here in 20 minutes?"

"Of course," I replied, hanging up the phone and trying to

wake myself up, knowing it was going to be a long eight-hour shift in the emergency room.

It had been almost a year since the Towers collapsed. While thoughts of what I saw on that autumn morning still wafted through my mind from time to time, I was beginning to heal. I could feel my heartbeat again. The New York firefighters of Engine 15, Ladder 18 had unknowingly taught me not to hold on to trauma or define myself by my pain or suffering, but rather by my strength. It was what made me want to start volunteering in the emergency room.

In the months after September 11th, I learned that we don't always get second chances in life, so I knew I had better make the first ones count every day. I put on my hospital badge. As I left my apartment, I realized I was no longer in that liminal space. I had put my old life behind me. I stepped out onto the street, and into who I had become.

LOVE

CHRIS JOSEPH

I woke up with a jolt.

It was a jarring feeling, one my brain instantly received but was unable to process quickly.

I didn't know what time it was or where I was, and I didn't know if I'd just had a dream or a nightmare.

I turned my head to look at the clock next to my bed and couldn't find it.

Damn it.

Where was I?

Scanning the room with confusion in the late-night blackness, I concluded I wasn't in my bed, nor was I at home.

I looked over and saw a woman sleeping in the same bed to the immediate right of me.

I realized I was at Susie's.

Susie, the love of my life, my long-time girlfriend of over four years at the time.

I stared at her. She was snoring girlishly, oblivious to my thoughts and perhaps even my presence. In my momentary confusion, I was envious of her. She was still sound asleep.

When I finally found my cell phone to check the time, it was a little after 1 am.

❦

I've never been a good sleeper. When I was a kid, I'd almost always be up at the crack of dawn to have breakfast with my dad and read the sports section in the *Los Angeles Times*.

As I got older, my early-to-rise habits morphed into waking up even earlier. My first job after graduating from the University of California, Riverside in 1981 was in downtown Los Angeles with the Unocal Corporation as an environmental engineer. It was a wonderful way to start my career and all was well and good, except my then-girlfriend and I were living in Grand Terrace, over an hour away from my new job, because she was finishing nursing school in San Bernardino.

Every weekday back then, I'd be up at 4 am. I'd eat breakfast, shower, throw on a suit and tie, and drive to a parking lot a few miles away where I joined a vanpool for the long drive to downtown LA.

I became used to waking up that early, even if I went to bed late. I would rarely use an alarm clock; my internal clock just knew what time to wake up.

On top of that, I hadn't been blessed with a body or brain that adapted well to sleeping pills or supplements. Either they didn't help me sleep better or, if they did, they came with unpleasant side effects.

And don't even get me started on how the aging process causes me to wake up at least one to two times in the middle of the night to have to go to the bathroom.

❦

In October 2016, at the age of 59, four months before this incident of waking up in the middle of the night at Susie's, I was shocked to learn that I had third-stage pancreatic cancer. The cancer diagnosis had instigated tremendous fear, a fear I was still suffering from that night at Susie's a few months later. A third-stage pancreatic cancer diagnosis is one thing, but when the subsequent treatment did not work and the chemotherapy itself was poisoning and killing my body—well, that was a fear that was off the charts, a kind I had never experienced in my entire life.

I thought I was going to die, and soon. I wasn't in a good place—mentally, emotionally, spiritually, and certainly not physically.

Almost every single night during that period as I fell asleep, I would obsessively scare myself about my imminent, agonizing and premature death.

⚜️

Between the time I got my cancer diagnosis and the night I woke up startled at Susie's, I had turned 60 years old.

In the 35 years prior, I had been married twice, and had had many other short and medium-term relationships before and in between both marriages. Because I'm human (and have occasionally suffered from a fragile ego), I also had a few one-night stands sprinkled in here and there.

Yet throughout my adult relationship history, I never felt I had a firm grasp on love. To be able to accept and give love without fear. Without conditions. Without judgment.

I never fully gave of myself out of fear of getting hurt, for fear that if someone *really* got to know me, they wouldn't love me.

They couldn't love me, I screamed at myself relentlessly. *I wasn't worthy and didn't deserve it.* After I convinced myself no one could love me, I inevitably found a way to leave the relationship. When I first heard Rosanne Cash sing, "Those who love can't get near me; those who don't are moving in," I cringed—I knew she was describing someone like me.

How could anyone *love me?* That inner voice was loud, powerful, and sometimes destructive, and I lived with it for a long, long time. What did love even mean?

I was convinced that you could put 25 people in a room, ask them that question, and get a bunch of different answers. And I didn't think I would ever come to know what true love with a partner really meant.

To be clear: I'm talking about relationship love. I've got two teenage boys, and I truly love them unconditionally—even in the moments when they are driving me nuts and I want to throttle them. But loving another person who isn't your offspring is something entirely different.

৩৯৩

As my brain fog cleared that night at Susie's, I tried to remember what had occurred while I was asleep that had caused me to awaken with a start.

After a few minutes, I recalled that the dream was, in part, about my imminent death from pancreatic cancer—and amazingly, I was somewhat comfortable with it. It was an acceptance of death, if you will—or at least, a partial acceptance.

But the bigger takeaway from the dream was about the woman lying next to me, and what I had learned from her.

It came to me in my dream that Susie, during the course of our four-year relationship, had taught me about love.

Susie had taught me that love was a verb, that it required hard work and effort.

She knew that love required loyalty. It required perseverance. Love needed patience and forgiveness, a willingness to accept that your mate wasn't perfect and was never going to be. It meant being able to accept and receive love, and to give love unconditionally.

Susie didn't teach me this through words, but rather by example. By living it. It's just who she is. For example, whenever we had one of our rare fights, it was more often Susie who was the calmer presence, who knew how to talk me down, who kept me from my usual *I have to get the fuck out of here* mentality.

I don't know if she's always been that way, but I know she learned these concepts well before I did.

I had been experiencing the way Susie loved for four years, but it wasn't until that night that I could fully feel what it was like to let love in, and to know and accept that she loved me.

I had learned to trust the love that she was giving me, to feel it, and even to embrace it. And I learned how to love Susie fiercely and unconditionally in return.

And I learned to let my guard down. As the saying goes, "Feel the fear and do it anyway." I was able to get past my fears.

After I realized what my dream was about that night, I realized that I had accomplished what I had been put on earth to do: to learn how to love.

In my dream, I knew that I was dying, and the reason I had accepted my imminent death (at least in part) was because I had finally learned the lesson I was supposed to learn in this life.

I was at peace with all of it. That early morning at Susie's—even after I woke up—I remained convinced I was going to die soon. I was sad and scared, but I was also relieved and enlightened.

At about 1:30 or so that morning, I fell back asleep and woke up later at a normal hour—well, a normal hour for me, which was around 4:30 am.

When I was wide awake again, I was so excited to tell Susie what had come to me a few hours before that I felt like a little kid. After I woke her up (I couldn't help myself), I started telling her about the dream and how revelatory it had been for me. It had been an epiphany.

As the words came spilling out of my mouth, I could see that Susie (especially in her very groggy state) couldn't quite understand what I was saying. That was on me because I wasn't exactly sure how to say it, either.

I couldn't remember the details of the dream, I told her, just the lessons I learned from it, and that my world had been flipped on its head.

I think she understood, but to this day, over four years later, I'm still not sure.

❧

Thankfully, my death from pancreatic cancer was not as imminent as I thought it was in my dream. I'm still around, living, and even thriving with cancer.

That said, even today, I occasionally struggle with issues of self-worth, and sometimes, I find myself wondering why and how someone—anyone—could love me. It has never completely disappeared, and it could be something I grapple with the rest of my life (though hopefully less so).

More often than not, however, the better part of me—the enlightened side—knows that the dream that night was at least partially real and true: I had learned how to give and receive love, even in an imperfect way.

MY WAY ISN'T ALWAYS THE RIGHT WAY

SAMANTHA PERKINS

I lay in bed with the blue light from my telephone screen lighting up the room. My husband was sound asleep next to me and I didn't want to wake him. He was so tired of hearing about the issues I was having. It was 1 am and I was in a manic frenzy trying to find a solution on the internet that would help me. I searched every post from Instagram influencers and on random blogs for a fix. I hated going to doctors.

Since I'd stopped drinking four years before, I had decided to live a raw life. Instead of calling my doctor every time I got a sinus infection or weird rash, I preferred to Google my symptoms to make sure there wasn't a more natural home remedy to try first. Most of the time this worked, but sometimes I fell down rabbit holes. I made herb concoctions recommended to me by people on the internet, hoping that I had properly diagnosed myself. This time, it wasn't working. I was left with no choice but to put my phone down and promise myself to make an appointment in the morning. I needed help.

As I opened the glass doors to the waiting room the next day, I felt overwhelmed. It was crowded, and even though this was the middle of the pandemic, almost every seat was taken. I stood in line to check in while TVs in every corner blared *The Today*

Show so loudly that it was hard to focus. When I got to the front of the line, the secretary behind the desk asked me the usual questions, but my mask felt suffocating and I was already flustered, so I accidentally gave her the wrong address. I hoped this wasn't a preview of what my appointment would be like.

As I looked around the room, I couldn't believe where I was. I had made a dozen appointments over the years but had always canceled. I would call and let the secretary know that I didn't have childcare or "something at work" came up and I "couldn't get away." I would reschedule in an effort to oblige her requests, but I knew that when I got the reminder call, I would find an excuse not to go. This particular doctor was the worst. I hated undressing, putting my feet in those weird stirrups, and being totally exposed. I feared I might have a panic attack.

The mix of anxiety, pride, and a faulty belief system kept me away from this place as long as possible. I was terrified to ask for help. For one, I had just written a book on how much my mental health had improved since I stopped drinking. I was afraid that if I told my doctor what was going on, it might mean I was not as healed as I had hoped. I didn't want to be a fraud.

As I sat waiting for my name to be called, I contemplated leaving. I was sitting so close to the door that it would be easy for me to slip out without anyone noticing. My leg was shaking so hard that I thought it might dislocate and hop away, and I chewed on the inside of my cheek. I was just about to gain enough courage to walk out when I remembered a few weeks ago I'd spent the whole day crying. It had been a beautiful sunny day, but I could barely pull myself out of bed. I didn't want to live like this. I needed to see the doctor. *Just stay calm. Tell her your symptoms,* I whispered to myself.

"Samantha Perkins?" the nurse called loudly.

I bolted to the door, aware that I was probably moving too fast.

In the room, the nurse weighed me and took my blood pressure.

"So your hormones are feeling a little out of whack?" she asked. I opened my mouth and tried to find a coherent sentence that would aptly explain what was going on, but then tears rushed to my eyes.

"Everything's wrong!" I blurted out.

"Okay," she said sweetly.

Dammit! I took a few deep breaths and managed to find some coherent thoughts. My PMS symptoms were intense. My mood was totally unstable for two weeks of every month. During those two weeks, I cried constantly and lay in bed thinking about everything that was wrong in the world.

I felt personally responsible for things that were out of my control, like childhood hunger and global warming. I was so depressed that I had to cancel social obligations and could barely work. I felt rage with no warning, which left me snapping at my kids or yelling at my husband while shaking with anger. I told the nurse about the time I almost asked my husband to take me to a crisis center to be institutionalized but then started my period and felt better within minutes. I told her I felt crazy.

"Okay," she said again, just as sweetly as the first time. "Let's go to the consultation room. You won't need an exam today."

Oh, thank God, I thought. My heart rate slowed immediately. I followed her into the room and eased into a soft seat next to a desk that held a computer. I was relieved to be fully clothed and with no beeping machines in sight. I knew it would be easier to describe my symptoms if I weren't wearing an itchy paper robe while laying on my back with my feet in the air.

When the doctor arrived, she asked me a few questions and since I was calm, I could answer accurately. Within minutes, she had diagnosed me with Premenstrual Dysphoric Disorder (PMDD) and offered a solution: "How would you feel about taking Prozac for two weeks a month?"

Ugh. Prozac? I thought. Obviously, I'd heard of the medication. Everyone had heard of Prozac. It's what was used to treat depression a long time ago before more advanced medications were developed. I thought that she must be really behind on her research if *this* was her idea of help. My face said it all.

"I know it's 'old school,' but patients say that it works for treating PMDD," she explained.

I couldn't remember the last time I'd taken even a pain reliever. I used lavender oil to help with headaches. I took hot baths with Epsom salt to rid myself of congestion. My skincare products were made of natural ingredients that could mostly be found in fields. My deodorant was a concoction of baking soda and coconut oil (which was ineffective, but I refused to switch back to Secret). I'd banned the people in my household from eating a certain cheese cracker because I was terrified of side effects from some of the chemically engineered ingredients.

I'd even learned to whip up homemade elixirs to treat my depression and anxiety, but like my deodorant, they hadn't been very effective. It was clear that I had not understood what I'd been treating. The doctor explained that PMDD was a severe negative reaction in the brain to the natural rise and fall of estrogen and progesterone. It was a suspected cellular disorder, which I was now realizing probably couldn't be cured with lavender oil and kale smoothies.

I remembered that I had read some things about PMDD during one of my frantic searches for help. The symptoms matched my current experience, but when I saw that one of the major treatment options was taking an antidepressant, I put it out of my head as an option. I had been down that road before, and the side effects were debilitating. Besides, I was living an *all-natural* life now.

I didn't know how to respond. It felt pointless to get into my "all-natural" spiel. I already knew that if those things had worked, I wouldn't be here to begin with. To her, trying the medication seemed like an obvious solution. I guess it was a combination of defeat, exhaustion, and desperation that led me to simply ask, "Do you think it will work?"

"I think it's worth trying. Lots of patients with PMDD have had success," she said.

"Okay!" I said overly enthusiastically, not sure if I would actually take it. In the past when doctors had given me prescriptions, I often tossed them in the trash.

I thanked her and walked out of the office to my car feeling numb. I was in a daze, repeating the word *Prozac* with each click of my boots on the parking garage floor. Exhaust fumes filled the air and while normally, I might have held my breath, I thought: *What was the point now? Pretty soon I would be ingesting chemicals.* I took a deep inhale.

In the car, I reached into my bag and grabbed my phone and started down that familiar rabbit hole again. I Googled: *What are the side effects of Prozac? Can Prozac cause a heart attack? Will Prozac kill me? Do celebrities take Prozac? Does Prozac cause blood clots? Can you have fun while taking Prozac? Will Prozac make me feel like a zombie? Will Prozac cure me?*

I realized that I probably should have asked the doctor a few more questions before leaving her office.

According to the internet, Prozac would either kill me or cure me. I stared out the window contemplating the appointment. I thought back to when I had debilitating anxiety. I had tried everything to heal it. I drank smoothies and went for long runs. I read self-help books and attended therapy. I ate all the right foods and prioritized sleep. I worked endlessly to try to rid myself of the mental anguish. I said that I would try anything to get relief. But that wasn't entirely true. I didn't want to give up drinking. I thought that would be the one thing that would be too hard, too damaging to my social life, too complicated, and too boring. I was wrong. Quitting drinking was the single most effective intervention I had ever tried. It solved most of my anxiety and a lot of other life issues within a matter of months.

What if taking Prozac would have the same results? What if I was wrong about chemicals being too dangerous? What if my brain needed the help of Prozac to function properly? I realized that maybe I was making things too hard. Maybe my way of doing things wasn't always the right way. Things in life were not so black and white. I had two choices: continue to live with this PMDD, sacrificing half of my life to this horrible disease, or try taking the medication.

I put my car in reverse and backed out of the garage. I didn't know if taking an antidepressant was going to work. But I did know that I had been wrong before. I drove to the pharmacy, hoping that this was going to be one of those times.

FUCKING PENCIL

BLAINE GRAY

Bam, bam, bam! The bullets slam into the giant tree I'm
hiding behind so hard that the ground shakes. A thought
races through my mind: *If I make it out of this alive, I'm going to do
everything I ever wanted to do. I will never, ever again take anything
for granted.*

In retrospect, it was an odd thought to have at that exact
moment. It all happened a few days before Christmas in 1989,
amid the ruins of a 500-year-old Spanish fort on the Panama
Canal. I was crouching behind an enormous ancient tree as an
American soldier in a Humvee emptied his 50-caliber machine
gun directly at me. I had pushed this memory so far down that it
didn't bubble up in my consciousness again until nearly 30 years
later in January 2017.

I'm in a beige chair in a beige office deep in Chatsworth,
California. Nancy, my new therapist, is doing eye movement
desensitization and reprocessing (EMDR) on me. I'm now
thinking about the first time I kissed a man on the lips as she
waves a pencil laterally—back and forth, back and forth. She
stops every couple of minutes to ask what I'm feeling. My replies
include:

"You're a fraud."

"I'm annoyed."

"This pisses me off."

Nancy nods and asks me to envision the combat experiences that brought me to this point. This resistance continues for several sessions until one day, I feel the rubbery limbs of a dead man covered in blood as he slips through my grasp and plops to the ground. I was back in Panama.

I had enlisted at age 17, searching for adventure, and was in boot camp while my peers graduated high school. I became a combat medic assigned to a reconnaissance platoon in the 82nd Airborne. In December 1989, our unit was on DRF1—Division Readiness Force. It meant being ready to deploy anywhere in the world in less than two hours. It also meant not drinking, always being on high alert, and carrying a pager to the movies—which is where I am, watching *Christmas Vacation,* when I get the alert.

We receive live ammo and grenades along with our mission brief in 18-degree weather on the tarmac of Pope Air Force Base, North Carolina. Our mission is to take the Torrijos International Airport in Panama and, if successful, move to a second follow-on mission. We were to be dropped onto the tarmac and would go from there. We would be parachuting into a war zone on what was to be only the 17th combat jump in US history.

After far too short a flight, the pilots divert from the airport and drop to 500 feet over the jungle to avoid the battle raging on the tarmac below. The C-141 airplanes we're jumping from cannot stay airborne under a certain speed far beyond the 138-mph maximum for parachuting. Under normal circumstances, planes had to be at or below 130 mph for paratroopers to safely make a jump; otherwise, the shock could knock them out or rip their parachutes in half.

The jumpmaster shouts over the noise of the engines: "Stand up! Hook up!"

We attach our ripcords to a cable above our heads. Packed tight, we pitch forward and back as the pilot struggles to keep the perfect balance of speed and power for the jump. As we approach the drop zone, the red light flashes. Barely able to move from the weight of our rucksacks, weapons and ammo, we stumble towards the door. The jumpmaster, who makes sure everyone exits safely before jumping himself, has to shove us out sideways.

As I hurtle towards the jungle below, I take in the following: first, half of the airplanes are missing. Second, and far more importantly, green bullet tracers are everywhere as the Rangers below fight with the Panamanian Defense Forces (PDF). Third, I just hit the top of the triple canopy jungle with my shoulder. Still horizontal, I'm dragged into the canopy sideways.

As I slam into the jungle floor, I don't feel the damage to my back and knee that will haunt me forever. I realize it is steam-room-hot, 100 degrees and 98 percent humidity—a stark contrast to the 18-degree North Carolina weather (that I later find out caused half the planes to ice up and abandon the mission).

In the absolute darkness of the jungle, glow sticks mark the equipment dropped in with us. It looks like a magical fairyland, only with bullets. The dense jungle muffles the gunshots and makes everything seem distant. Still dazed, I struggle to unpack my weapon as enemy fighters fleeing the battle run right past me. Am I supposed to shoot them? I'm not sure. Either way, they're long gone by the time I have my weapon ready.

Just before dawn, we finally assemble on the airport tarmac and wait for helicopter transport to arrive. One of the Black Hawks in the approaching formation pitches forward and almost takes out the whole group. A sniper has shot the pilot, but he holds it together long enough to land without crashing. As the reconnaissance platoon, our follow-on mission was to take the PDF Special Forces' headquarters in Panama Viejo. We would be at least a day or more ahead of the other troops, operating with limited support. The helicopters skim just above the waves as day breaks over the Gulf of Panama. Our landing zone is a small strip of sand barely large enough for one helicopter at a time.

As we hover, waiting to land, a large group of civilians gathers below waving American flags. I wonder how I can hear insects buzzing over the roar of the helicopter. Then I realize the buzzing isn't insects; the PDF Special Forces had changed into civilian clothes and were shooting at us from the crowd below. The helicopters wouldn't be able to land, and we'd have to jump out a few feet above the muddy canal. Half the guys drop into chest-high mud; I'm lucky enough to land on the tiny strip of sand. We're immediately in a full firefight, battling our way off the strip of sand to the street above.

Meanwhile, Nancy is still doing her stupid fucking EMDR pencil bullshit—back and forth, back and forth.

The pencil is doing its job because *boom*—I feel myself blown to the side of my beige chair and my ears begin to ring. I realize that ringing has been with me ever since that morning in Panama, where I am now.

Our squad is trapped on that damn strip of sand. Another firefight rages on the street above. Suddenly, mortar rounds explode on the beach, each one closer as they target us. The sand absorbs much of the impact and the shrapnel. Our backs are at a 30-foot sea wall; there's no place for us to go.

We watch as the mortars creep closer with nowhere to hide. One hits less than 10 feet away from me and the fear that should be present is absent. We've been awake for almost 48 hours at this point, and our emotions are dulled. We know they have us dead to rights. Crouching low, we wait. Suddenly, out of nowhere, an Apache helicopter hovers above us and fires an intense volley of rockets, ending the attack seconds before the last mortar is fired. Relief is temporary, though; once the firefight ends, panicked screams of "medic" ring out. As a combat medic, you get the double-fuck of both shooting and treating the wounded.

I climb up to the street and find a large American car riddled with bullets with several dead (or soon-to-be-dead) young men in it. The car rests in a small ditch in a field. We have to stand in the ditch to access the doors at eye level. The driver is dead, shot through the left eye and missing the back of his head. I pull him out to get to the others.

In my therapist's office, it's *his* bloody, rubbery dead limbs that I feel slip through my hands as he falls to the ground. There's an indescribable sound that a bloody wet body makes when it hits the ground. The dead men in the car have no weapons on them and all I can think is: *I hope we didn't just kill innocents.*

A sergeant I know approaches and explains they had attacked earlier; recognizing their car when they returned, our forces attacked. To my relief, they find multiple weapons in the trunk. That same sergeant approaches the driver's body and sticks his finger through the hole in the man's skull, marveling at the damage. At that moment, I realize there are three types of people in combat: those who run away from gunfire, those who run towards it and those who thrive in it. Even today, I have to resist the urge to run towards gunfire and chaos.

Back and forth. Back and forth. The pencil stops.

"What are you feeling?"

"Angry. Sad. Fuck!"

I had never told anyone about kissing the wounded soldier, not for any particular reason. I never told anyone much of anything. Certainly, I hadn't told Nancy. He was a soldier whose machine gun fired while he was cleaning it.

The bullets had ricocheted off the adobe walls and gone back into his body, lodged against his spine. We were far ahead of our unit, so we had to tear off a wooden door to use as a stretcher and transport him to the helipad on the hood of a stolen Jeep we hot-wired.

Since we were both from Phoenix, he insisted that I keep pushing the morphine even though a far more qualified physician's assistant was on hand. As we waited for a dust-off helicopter to arrive, we sang Oingo Boingo's "Dead Man's Party," the only song we both knew, to keep him conscious.

In between grunts and him begging for his mother, he asked me to kiss him. I leaned over and kissed his forehead. He looked up at me and said, "Kiss me on the lips, doc." So much went through my mind at that moment. *Was this gay?* The others were watching me. *What about AIDS?* I was covered in scratches from the jump and had at least five men's blood and brain matter on me. I took a deep breath, wiped the blood spatter from his face and kissed him on the lips. When the helicopter finally arrived, the officers on board refused to exit for us to load him in. It was incredibly gratifying as we shoved the wooden door in place so hard that it knocked one of the colonels out of the chopper onto the ground.

A couple of days after taking control of the compound, another infantry company arrived in Humvees. We'd been taking sniper fire the whole time, but when the Humvees approached, the PDF sniper turned on them. The soldiers thought the gunfire was from our position, so they stormed the fort, guns blazing. I made eye contact with the 50-cal gunner on top of a Humvee as he pivoted the barrel towards me. Time stopped as I realized he was going to shoot me.

I dove behind the massive tree that absorbed countless rounds, protecting me. Even with the vow I make to never take anything for granted and go after my dreams, nothing prepares me for the next few minutes. One of the soldiers from the Humvees has been shot in the head. He's dead; his body just doesn't know it yet. Even with help on the way, there's no hope. I sit with him and smoke a cigarette as he dies. I hold his hand as he takes his final breath overlooking the ships backed up on the Panama Canal.

The pencil swims back into view, no longer clouded by memories. I'm exhausted, shattered from the mix of adrenaline and emotion it's brought forth. What now? I'd spent years repressing these emotions and now they were consuming me. In the days, weeks, months that followed those sessions, a sense of hopelessness blanketed my life.

One day while driving, a thought cut through the mental roar. All those years ago, I'd given myself a light at the end of a very long, dark tunnel: *If I make it out of this alive, I'm going to do everything I ever wanted to do. I will never, ever again take anything for granted.*

Even today it guides me.

WAVES

PETER AVILDSEN

*Z*uma is perfect. The continent ends at Zuma and coastal mountains plunge into the Pacific, forming a shelf of sand a mile wide.

The beach at Zuma curves gently south and ends at Point Dume, the northernmost point of Santa Monica Bay. An unending stream of waves break on the long, shallow shore, some a foot high and some ten feet high, a dream for surfing and bodyboarding.

At Zuma last month, on the tail end of a long ride into shore on my bodyboard, I had a perfect moment. I was at the north end of the beach where the kids learn to surf, catching slow, easy waves with long finishes, sliding 50 yards across water only inches deep.

Fully present with the sun and the waves, I was transfixed by the ocean curling beneath the front of my board. The bright afternoon sun sparkling through the spray took me back to the countless hours I spent on boats in my childhood. I loved to ride in the front, getting lost in the mystery of the infinite wake the boat would throw as it cut through the sea.

When my bodyboard scraped up on the beach I slid off, turned, and kneeled to face the incoming waves, letting memories from those early years wash over me. Time near the water was the best part of my childhood. My family seemed happy there and I felt safe, although now I know I wasn't.

This is how I imagined writing about an epiphany would start. I would find a moment of insight and clarity, illuminated by natural beauty and wonder. A moment like the evening in Paris I crossed the threshold into the Sainte-Chapelle as the golden rays of the setting sun streamed through the cobalt blue stained-glass windows, the brilliant tones of a trumpet piercing the cathedral's vast, dusky silence.

Or maybe it would be wistful and sad: how I found love and how I lost it, or memories of the ones I loved who are no longer here. Of loves I failed to cherish, or hopes and dreams I could not acknowledge, or those I saw and still let slip away.

Fuck! is what spilled out onto the page when I began to write.

I tried to think of something beautiful and what came to mind was a day in Germany. A late autumn afternoon with the pale sun glinting on the broad surface of the Rhine, the peaceful sounds of water softly lapping against the rocky shore.

That day I was four months into my 26th year, and they had been the best four months of my life. That day, October 6, 1987, was the worst day of my life.

That day I woke up to a voice from the school where I was studying in Koblenz, telling me they would connect me with my mother in Chicago. She said my little sister was dead.

That day I was cast adrift, exiled from a world where I could make sense of life. I wandered the banks of the Rhine for hours, looking for solace and finding none.

Fuck! You couldn't even keep Katrina alive for four months?

My epiphany today is that I am deeply, achingly angry, even if it is way too late to be angry. I am 60 years old. I cannot go back and live a different life, but I want a different past. I want things to have been different, to have been able to make different choices. I want to believe life could have been different.

Today I am looking at a tiny black and white photo of me

and Katrina in the bath. I might have been four and she three, soap bubbles on our chins. I always loved that picture, but what I see today is a girl who was not held tightly enough and a boy who was not seen.

I shared the photo with a friend recently and they saw my amblyopia right away. I only became conscious of it five years ago and was shocked when the family and friends I asked said they had always seen my "lazy" eye. I did not know it was noticeable because no one ever mentioned it, and no one ever did anything about it.

I know it was a problem worth fixing and one that could be fixed because my oldest brother had worn an eye patch to treat his amblyopia. It was the 1960s, not the 1690s. My family had plenty of resources, and yet no one noticed how I was looking at them. Now I know why seeing what is right in front of me has always been hard.

Fuck. That is what comes now when I look at that picture. Why were we there if no one was able to care for us? That is an epiphany I am still waiting on.

I thought I loved epiphanies, that I lived for epiphanies, that I never met an epiphany I didn't like. But I do not like this one.

I thought epiphanies connected me with something greater than myself. I remember loving that feeling even at an early age, lying on a bright green summer lawn looking up at a soft blue sky with a warm yellow sun and puffy white clouds. That feeling of connection is as real in this moment as it was on that day 50 years ago.

I live for that feeling and have searched for it many ways: smoking pot day and night, dropping acid like candy, being born again, practicing energetic karate and tai chi and yoga, sailing, hiking, swimming, diving, and bodyboarding. I have relished special bites, savored exquisite sips, explored the world around me, and read words, so many words.

I was always searching for something breathtaking or moving or extraordinary. Always looking for the exquisite moment, the flash of green as the sun melts into the sea, the moment where I would find myself amazed to be alive and part of this infinite universe.

When I started writing this, I sifted through my memories for one of those moments. But then I did what writers do and left the writing to do some reading and ended up somewhere else entirely.

I found that epiphany comes from the Greek word ἐπιφάνεια, which means to reveal, and transcendence is from the Latin *transcendere*, to climb beyond. An epiphany shines a light on your world, shows you what you have not been able to see, while transcendence is an experience beyond the world you are in.

I have always loved transcendent moments, but for a long time, I was moving too fast to take in the epiphanies that came my way. Perhaps I was a little scared of what might be hidden.

I have learned to slow down when there is something just out of view, to spend time waiting to see what it might be and to trust that whatever I find will be something I want to know. Five years ago, I began a process of uncovering something I didn't know was hiding.

It started with noticing an occasional pain in my lower back. It was nothing significant, but I didn't want to wait until it was something I could not dismiss. I mentioned it to my doctor and she directed me to an amazing physical therapist.

That was the start of a journey to rebuild my physical core. It has meant changing the way I sit and stand and walk and sleep, becoming aware of all the ways I move and how I avoid movement.

Five years ago, I also began to rebuild my emotional and energetic core, though I did not realize it at the time. And amid all that, I had the epiphany that made it possible to keep going, to be willing to change everything.

I realized the pain in my back was a sensation. It was nerves communicating information about how I was extending and deforming tissues, what my range of motion was, what condition the muscles and bones and nerves were in. I realized I could welcome that information. I could treasure it, and it would guide me on my healing journey.

Names have a power of their own, beyond what they are attached to. What we call a thing creates the frame for how we view it. Five years ago in the physical therapist's office, I realized I did not have to call those sensations pain. I could call them information.

Calling it information gave me a choice. Information made no demands, only provided an awareness. Once I understood the pain as information, I could learn to accept it and build my capacity for feeling the sensations.

I learned to feel what needed to be felt and acknowledge whatever came, learned to listen, to make room, to welcome all the feelings and let them come all the way through without judging them. A sensation is not good or bad or right or wrong; it is just information, and I can choose what to do with information.

As I started to feel, I realized how much effort and energy I put into not feeling, how afraid I was of feeling pain. How worried I was that the information would be something bad.

Five years ago, I changed how I looked at pain. And at the same time, I literally changed the way I see.

In the same month I started physical therapy, I took a workshop about art and money, about making a living doing what you love. I was expecting a presentation, a whiteboard with a circle divided into different colored segments, and advice about managing my time. Instead, we did a series of meditations and somatic exercises.

I was shocked to find myself connecting with a wrenching pain in my heart, and an anger that had been buried deep. All the energy I had spent denying and suppressing pain and fear and anger was released and expressed. It was exhilarating and exhausting.

Afterwards, the other participants all commented on how different I looked, which puzzled me. When I asked them what that meant, they told me I was "looking" differently, that both my eyes were focused together. I had not realized that my "lazy" eye was a thing that other people noticed, or that I could choose to look with both eyes.

I went searching for more information because I was ready for a different experience. I found a story that led me to a great optometrist, and a whole journey of understanding eyes and vision and how much volition I have over how and what I see.

And every time Dr. Nakata checks my eyes, she asks, "Are you doing the exercises I gave you to make your eyes converge?" And I have to say, "No."

I have not done those fucking eye exercises because I learned a long time ago to hate exercise. To resist making myself stronger, better, faster. To lose and not to want to win.

Fuck that. That's my epiphany today.

I have found other ways to heal, other ways to change, to feel more, learn more. Glasses that help me to focus my eyes, teachers who shared different ways to see, ways that don't feel like exercise, the way practicing a headstand or hiking or bodyboarding does not feel like going to the gym.

Some days I think about how my eyes are working, some days I forget or do not want to bother, and some days my eyes work on their own and the stereo vision kicks in automatically. When that happens, it feels like I have woken up in the middle of a 3D movie.

I see the distance between the leaves and branches and tree trunks right in front of me, how they exist in relation to each other and the hillside behind them, and it stops me. I want to turn to the nearest person and whisper, *"Do you see that?! What's going on?!"* And I'm just seeing what most people always see.

And some days I write. I'm fucking writing. I can hardly believe it; it is amazing in and of itself just to put pen to paper. I feel so alive when the words pour out, like this is what I was meant to do. When that happens, I can write and write and feel like I might never stop.

And today I am living better. Not how I would have lived if everything had been different, but the best I can based on what I know today, based on going deep inside and listening.

The longer I have stayed with this epiphany, that I can choose how to understand my experience based on the information I'm receiving, the more the light reveals. I see how I designed my life to avoid feeling what my body was telling me, chose postures and activities and environments that protected me from feeling.

I see how I designed my life to avoid feeling the emotions I was afraid of. I see how trying to avoid some feelings meant I numbed myself to all feelings. I see now I was raised in a family that did not acknowledge what we were feeling, that I was raised in a culture that was designed not to acknowledge or value feeling.

Now I am on a journey to receive the information I learned to avoid. To feel all my feelings, and to trust that they are providing information I need and want.

There are epiphanies I am still waiting for. I want to connect to the memories of my parents' love and care without denying the pain and hurt that was there. I want to know I am good right where I am.

I know I am good when I am in the water. For the last 30 years, I have plunged into the chest-high waves of the numbingly cold Pacific for fun. I love throwing myself into a wave, smacking into it with all my energy without wondering whether I am too much. The waves can take it, and most of the time, I can handle what the waves throw back.

And when I catch a wave at the perfect moment, a bolt of joy runs through me and I find myself laughing as I fly towards the shore. I come out of the water feeling every inch of my body, exhilarated and exhausted. The light sparkles on the water, and I am eager to see what else may be revealed.

B IS FOR BACKWARDS

BETH ROBINSON

I t's a lovely June day. It's continually surprising that it's summer after four days spent mostly in the hospital.

Mom's room looked out onto an interior courtyard. Sun filtered down from skylights several stories up, but the room still felt like it was in a windowless basement. For most of those days, we sat on the sofa and in the armchair in that room, watching the ventilator breathe for her, watching nurses come in and out and fuss with tubes and monitors and bags. It seemed futile to me.

The morning after they brought her in, I called the doctor. "I know you can't tell me what's going to happen," I said, "but if it were your mother and your brother was in Los Angeles, would you call him and tell him to get on a plane?"

"The short answer," he said, "is yes."

There was a long answer too, but I knew what was happening —I had known for months.

It was weird to be in her house. Everything felt weird. She wasn't there. The house didn't quite feel like the place where we had gathered for holidays, with her grandchildren running up and down the basement stairs, the busyness of the kitchen, the smell of brisket. And we weren't there to visit or to celebrate. We were there to pass the time until her funeral.

And I was there to find a necklace I had made her. It was silver, with a large chunk of sparkly white druse in the middle, a rutilated quartz teardrop hanging from it, and a garnet, which was her birthstone, set on top. She told me how much people admired it when she wore it in Boca. I knew she loved telling them her daughter made it for her. I knew she loved telling me people admired it. It was a really nice piece, but it was more than that. Right then, it felt like the only palpable proof of our connection to each other, and I badly wanted to wear it to her funeral.

My sister-in-law Tina had flown in from LA by then. Together, we went up into my mother's closet and started looking through her jewelry. I set aside some pieces I wanted. Mostly pieces I had made or bought for her for Mother's Day, Chanukah, her birthday. There was always a wall between us, so we expressed our love by throwing jewelry and other accessories over it. The story of our relationship could be told in clothes and handbags and necklaces and pins and bracelets and rings.

My mother loved clothes that were elegant and clean and neat and, most importantly, that came pre-assembled in well-thought-out outfits. I loved expressing myself, mixing and matching in what my father used to call "costumes." But he once came to breakfast wearing plaid pants and a striped shirt and when I pointed it out, he looked down, shrugged indifferently, and went off to work. It was one of the worst moments of a sartorial career that ranged from unimaginative to memorably awful. So, I didn't really care what he said about my "costumes." My mother, however, had a way of looking me up and down without looking me in the face that was both irritating and crushing. I wasn't matched enough. I wasn't polished enough. I wasn't *her* enough. I wasn't enough.

"What?" I would ask.

"Oh, nothing."

My mother picked out my clothes for me until my senior year of high school when I traded in kilts, crewnecks, and penny loafers for a pair of khaki overalls I wore every chance I could. Then I went to art school. It was right after *Flashdance* came out and I wore sweat clothes I cut up and embellished with paint and beads.

After I washed out in both art school and the theater department, submarined by undiagnosed seasonal depression, I came home and resumed dressing like a regular citizen, married a suitable Jewish husband, and proceeded to have two children, and start drinking heavily in cropped slacks and floral twinsets.

After my divorce, I returned to my "costumes," and one day, while shopping with my mother, an exercise I loathed for reasons having entirely to do with guilt, anger, and a frustrating struggle with my own identity, she held up a pair of Western boot-style mules.

"How about these?" she asked hopefully.

They had stitched seams, a snip toe, and a stacked wooden heel. I couldn't have picked better. It was the first time she had picked something out for me that I had looked at and seen my style.

"Yeah, I like them," I said, surprised. I let her buy them for me and I let myself enjoy wearing them.

I was thinking about that and thinking about the love language of jewelry while I went through her things.

I was angry at her for starving herself to death. I had talked to her doctors. I knew she wasn't doing what she needed to do to stay alive, to keep up her strength so they could treat the lung disease that was killing her. She was steadily losing a pound a week and I was constantly pushing her to get a feeding tube. When she finally agreed to it, I was angry about her timing.

I had just started a new job and didn't have the time or energy to be a perfect daughter. She was dying, and it was partly because she hadn't done what her doctors had told her to do. She was doing it at a time that was really inconvenient for me, and I felt both angry and terribly guilty. I was there at the end, continually, but I still felt horrible about my stinginess and resentment. What had been eating at me for days was wondering if, when she died, she knew I loved her.

Grief and guilt and anger all chased each other around in my gut as I opened her neatly organized jewelry drawers.

What was I doing going through her things? The strangeness of us in her house without her, the odd unbalanced noise of us surrounding the empty silent spot of her, felt numb and raw at the same time. My skin hurt with grief.

I found a necklace I had hurriedly assembled as a birthday gift, an asymmetrical heart I had cut out of silver and strung on purple and green beads. It looked like something she would have bought herself at an art fair. I found pieces I had bought at art fairs, at my favorite galleries in Ann Arbor, pieces we'd designed together at my friend Nomi's bead store. I found the language in which I had said "I love you" to my mother over and over throughout the years. That's why she loved that drusy piece so much. I get it—my room is filled with everything my children have ever given me. They are my ultimate treasures, and that necklace was hers.

Tina and I pulled out travel bags full of jewelry looking for it. We looked through drawers. Mom's boyfriend, Gary, was sitting in their kitchen reading. I asked him if he'd seen it and he said that it might still be in Florida and that he would look around their condo when he got back if we didn't find it.

I found her wedding ring and her engagement ring. I thought Emma and Ruby might like to wear something of hers to the funeral too. In the complicated mess of all our mother, daughter, sister relationships, her relationship with my girls had been so wonderfully simple. She adored them and they adored her. I found the pinecone section pendant we ordered after she admired one Emma bought at a music festival. I set it aside for Emma to wear. I found some delicate chains with tiny pendants that I thought Ruby might like, including the gold "B" she often wore.

Different pieces reminded me of different occasions, and I wept. I wept because my mother was gone and because I didn't know if I had been a good daughter. I wept because it was too late to say *I'm sorry* or *I love you* or to get on a plane and fly to Florida and make her take care of herself.

She had told each of us that there were some specific pieces she wanted to go to her granddaughters and daughters-in-law, and we were sure she had made a list. We scoured her office but didn't find it.

So, each time Tina admired something or said that she remembered giving it to my mother, I said, "Take it." It felt right. I knew she wanted everyone to have something; we just didn't know what. Tina chose a set of gold stacking rings and a wide silver ring set with a large faceted citrine. I really liked that ring, but my mother's fingers, even when she was healthy, were much more slender than mine. She was, by nature, a more elegant creature than I am.

I sat at her makeup table with some of the travel bags which I had checked over and over, close to giving up. I had found lots of other pieces I could wear. I could wear the large copper and crystal tree-of-life pendant I had made her or the silver heart, but the drusy piece was the one I wanted. I knew it was special to her, that it meant something, that it connected us in some way, so it was the one piece that felt like it would bring her close to me.

"Is this it?" Tina asked from the closet.

I got up and went to look. It was. It had been in one of the bags and I had somehow missed it. I took it and hugged Tina, clasping it hard in one hand.

I wore it to the funeral. Emma wore the pinecone. Ruby

wore the gold "B." As we were leaving to go to the funeral, I looked at it and noticed I had put it on her backwards.

"Do you know what B stands for?" I asked.

"Barbara?"

"No, backwards."

She paused, then rolled her eyes and walked out to the car.

MY INTERVIEW WITH JOHN TRAVOLTA

JOHN FERREIRA

*S*o there I was, *sitting at a round table with John Travolta on my
left and some person interviewing us on the other side. I have no
idea what the interview was promoting, or even why I was there for
that matter. All I knew was I was sitting next to John!*
Hey! That's my name too!

🙰

Sigmund Freud called dream interpretation the "royal road" to
the unconscious. He claims these connections are not random
but rather "a fulfillment of a wish." The only thing I have in
common with John Travolta is our love of flying. So why in the
world did I dream about him? What wish am I trying to fulfill?

All I know is the nerve endings in my body are tingling with
excitement. It is 2:30 in the morning and I need to share the
dream I just had. I can't contain it!

I wake my girlfriend asking her permission to tell my story.
When she groggily agrees, I don't hesitate, quickly propping
myself up on my elbows and enthusiastically describing my realistic experience. She struggles to keep up with my animated
narrative.

I think we were supposed to talk about some upcoming movie, but that's not what I wanted to talk about. Forget John's movies. Forget his fame. I wanted to talk about flying! I couldn't wait 'til we got onto that subject.

Finally, the interviewer asked me a question about aviation. Yes! This is where I would really connect with John.

I pump my fist and the bed shakes. My girlfriend smiles through closed eyes. I continue.

The look on John's face! He lit up like a kid in a candy store—no, it was bigger! More like a child being surprised on their birthday, opening their eyes and seeing Disneyland for the first time.

There was some talk about flying a Qantas airplane and when asked if he had any other aviation dreams, he mentioned something about flying in space.

That's when I jumped in. "I've always wanted to fly into space. When I was younger and visualized an interview at United Airlines where I would be asked the question, 'Where do you see yourself in ten years?' I had a pre-made answer ready to go: 'Flying a United Airlines aircraft into space, of course.'"

When I was nine playing in the park, I'd stop to wave at the planes that departed San Francisco International. My friends would cover their ears as the deafening roar from the turbojets a couple of thousand feet above our heads shook the trees and reverberated in the pits of our stomachs.

With my head craned skyward and my right arm rapidly moving back and forth, they thought I was crazy—but I knew all the passengers were waving back. Being smaller in stature, I dreamed I'd eventually fly the biggest airplane, a 747, no longer being looked down on but looked up to.

I glance at my girlfriend. She still seems awake.

*I paused a minute, then I thought of my impossible dream to fly
in space and got even more excited. I may not be able to do it, but
I know John Travolta could!*

*Before the interviewer had a chance to ask his next question, I
added, "Hey, John. Maybe you should get a hold of Richard
Branson and see if you can fly one of the Virgin Galactic planes?
If anyone could do that, I know you could. That would be
AWESOME!"*

I love watching other people achieve their goals. It brings me
so much satisfaction to help someone accomplish their dreams.
Maybe that's why being a flight instructor, training captain and
check airman have been the most rewarding parts of my aviation
career.

I pause for a minute in my story. I think about how cool it
would be if John Travolta flew into outer space only because I
had planted the seed and given him the push to try and succeed.
It would be as if I had done it myself. My girlfriend opens her
eyes, acknowledging with a look that she is still listening and for
me to keep going.

*John didn't say anything, rapidly nodding his head—grinning,
calculating, the wheels in his brain definitely thinking about the
possibility.*

*The interviewer was about to speak again, but I cut him off. I
was just getting started.*

*"One of my favorite video clips was when Dick Clark inter-
viewed you on* American Bandstand *after you filmed* Saturday
Night Fever. *I think you were in your early 20s. He asked, 'If
you had time off, what would you do?' Man! You started talking*

about flying and I could see the excitement in your eyes and hear it in your voice. It always brings me back to how I feel about flying."

Then the interview panned to a video of Dick Clark talking to an extremely young John Travolta. I felt as if I was now watching everything on an old television. Dick Clark suggested there were probably a few women who might want to go flying with John—so cool how quickly TV producers can pull those videos up during a live interview.

The image on the TV returned to our interview, the camera shot zooming in on John's flushed face as he recollected. "I had forgotten about that," John said and laughed. He still has that big, toothy smile—you know, the one that draws in the ladies. I heard a few sigh in the studio audience.

Then I was back in the interview, sitting next to John, eagerly continuing, "And the children's book you wrote! Priceless! I loved it. It was as if you were Richard Bach writing about his experiences as a child."

John's face beams as I compare him to the famous aviation author who wrote Jonathan Livingston Seagull and other great flying stories.

John Travolta describes his love of flight in a fable he wrote for his family titled *Propeller One-Way Night Coach*. It's a story about an eight-year-old boy who turned his dream of flying into reality by planning a trip with his mother to fly from Newark to Los Angeles through a series of connections. It was the same excitement I experienced when I was 16 and had the rare opportunity to fly in a King Air from Palo Alto to Las Vegas.

I took my first flying lesson when I was 19, and my passion has only intensified since. As Leonardo da Vinci said, "Once you have tasted flight, you will forever walk the earth with your eyes turned skyward, for there you have been, and there you will long to return."

I pause a second to take a breath. My girlfriend nods, urging me to continue.

The interviewer seems extremely impatient. I took over his job and it's not going as he had planned. He clears his throat to get John's attention, then asks the hard question. The subject he really wanted to focus on. He asks how John's managing after the passing of his wife.

John's body language tells way more than his words or voice portray. That child-like joy, the abandon that comes when one expresses what they love the most in the world, is crushed in an instant. His shoulders hunch inward. I notice his knees shaking under the table. His eyes, once bright and cheery, now seem vacant and distant. And his smile is no longer genuine but forced. I see John focusing on his breathing, concentrating hard to maintain his composure as he stoically answers the interviewer's question.

I can't help it. I feel the energy shift and there's no way I can't let him know that it's okay to express grief. The interviewer doesn't seem to notice that John's vitality has dropped, continuing to focus on his loss. I understand the pain of losing someone you love.

Grief is a curious thing. It sneaks up on you when you least expect it. Takes you by surprise. One minute you're present, calm, relaxed. The next, it feels like you've been slammed by a freight train.

I was 33 when my biological father lost his battle to liver cancer. His oncologist gave him a few months to live, but he held on a couple more. In that narrow window, my ex and I brought his two-week-old granddaughter across the country so she could meet him, and so I could say goodbye. His mind was sharp, yet he was nearly skeletal, with an overly distended belly that looked nothing like the man I had seen a couple of years earlier.

I was 34 when my grandfather was admitted to a nursing home, no longer able to care for himself due to Alzheimer's. Here was a man whose body was healthy but had lost his mind, eventually no longer recognizing anyone. He was a gentle, intelligent, funny man, a mechanical engineer who loved Kermit the Frog. He mutated into an angry, cursing lunatic, no longer the person I'd idolized as a child. I was 35 when he died.

A few months later, my mother was diagnosed with ovarian cancer. She had a hysterectomy, a round of chemotherapy, and agreed to take a trial drug. Nothing worked. When asked to do a second round of chemotherapy, she declined, choosing hospice instead. A year after her original diagnosis, she too was gone, her body looking 20 years older than her actual age of 62.

I was 40 when I lost my stepfather to pancreatic cancer. My ex and I not only juggled parenting and our own lives, but we also managed my stepfather's home-based business and were his primary caretakers as the disease attacked and ravaged his body.

And yet, the combination of all those deaths never prepared me for the excruciating pain of separation and divorce, a feeling I can only describe as a slow ripping of the soul.

I know the agony of loss.

My girlfriend reaches out and grabs my hand as she feels the energy in my story shift.

John looks at me and I give him all the understanding and sympathy I can muster in my eyes as I look back. He takes a deep breath and pauses. I place my hand on his shoulder, followed by saying something so profound I don't know if I would have ever thought of it while awake:

"Grief is something we will all experience. For me, it's like standing at the water's edge on a beach. Grief is the pulling of the

water as it rushes back out to sea. We feel that tug on our bodies, threatening to take us with it. If we aren't careful, we can get knocked off balance and pulled away from the shore.

"It's when we no longer have that firm footing on solid ground that we start to panic and exhaust ourselves. Wave after wave crashes upon us and we pop up just long enough to take a breath before being knocked back down again. If we aren't careful, we can allow our grief to overwhelm and eventually drown us.

"Don't try to run from grief and yet, don't get too far out in the water that it takes over. Instead, embrace it, and stand with your feet firm on the sand, allowing the water to tug at your ankles. Allow yourself to experience grief without letting it overcome you."

My dream shifts. I'm standing on the seashore, my feet stable on the wet beach, grains of sand tickling my toes. I look down, feeling the warmth of the ocean around my ankles while watching the water swirl as it gently splashes onto the shore and gurgles back out to sea. I smell the salty air and hear the gulls screaming amongst one another.

I no longer experience a grief so deep that it feels like I'm drowning, gasping for air. I no longer feel the panic and fear I had when it seemed as if my whole world was collapsing around me. I feel a sense of peace, and yet the tug of the waves still reminds me not only of the diminishing pain, but the joys I experienced prior to the loss. The water reminds me that without the slight tug of grief, I wouldn't be able to experience the full joy life brings us.

The dream fades back to the interview. I see a tear in John's eyes. It's as if he had been standing on that beach right next to me experiencing on a deep, emotional level what I had just gone through. We're connected in a profound way.

There were more conversations with the interviewer. I don't remember what was said. Yet right before I woke up, John looked at me and told me he was writing an autobiography and because I was so well versed in my writing, he wanted me to help proof-read his work.

I'm not sure where that came from, but it sure did stroke my ego!

My girlfriend struggles to take in every word. I apologize for waking her, although I do ask if she heard or remembered anything I said. I'm still searching for validation. Some habits are still hard to break.

Peering through half lids, my girlfriend tries her hardest to be coherent and replies, "Something about an interview with John Travolta." A long pause and a sigh. "I'm sorry, honey. I don't remember. I think it's cute you're so excited. I feel blessed you'd want to share this with me. I can tell this dream means a lot to you and I hope you can remember it in the morning."

Her voice fades away, her eyes close, and she's back asleep, her breathing delicate and musical.

☙❧

A few days later, when I return home, I go straight to my book-case and grab my copy of *Propeller One-Way Night Coach*. I haven't read it in years. In fact, I don't think I've even read it to my girls. Has it really been since before the millennium? I brush off the dust and open to the first page. The Dedication:

> "This book is dedicated to my son Jett, whom I love more than life itself and my wife Kelly, who magically holds the key to Jett's first chapter and my second."

Wham! The freight train comes and slams me into the turbulent sea.

Closing my eyes, I acknowledge and embrace the feeling in

my body, no longer trying to hide from it nor allowing it to over-whelm me. I instinctively slow my breath, measured and rhyth-mic, like gentle waves lapping upon the shore. I feel the tension loosening, my energy dissipating. I continue to breathe deeply until I feel calmness settle in. I open my eyes, once again present in the world, as if I'm back on that beach standing ankle-deep in the water.

DO NOT CALL ME PERFECT

SARA ONEIL

My sister and I can fight. I'm talking battles that reality TV dreams are made of. But that's the thing with families, there's no need for sugar coating. If something needs to be said, it's said. Which is why reality television can't get enough of the family dynamic: it's juicy. I normally try not to fight with people I love because I'm so paranoid they will die, and the venom I poured will be my last memory. What if I tell someone to go fuck themselves and then they keel over and leave this earth? This terrifies me to my core.

Years ago, my sister and I had an epic battle. Like Oscar-winning as far as brawls go. The reason was the same as it always was: I was trying to control her, and she wanted me off her back. This was our lifelong theme, but on this particular night, we outdid ourselves and we both snapped. Our WWE-level catfight escalated to the point where we were surprised the police had not been called.

I wanted her to live life the way I thought she should. She felt controlled and judged. She screamed furiously:

"Sorry I can't be as perfect as you!"

My screeching reply as I fell to the floor dramatically while pointing a finger was:

"Don't EVER call me perfect!"

Tears. Anguish. Drama.

And scene.

You see, here's the thing: do not call me fucking perfect.

That, for me, is like leaving cold kittens outside. Unfathomable. Hearing the word "perfect" uttered as a description next to my name is worse than robbing me of every item I own. It touches that "this is your gaping wound" button—that annoying spot that either gets healed or loops back around for another standing ovation. Perfectionism has taken me down, and this is not an understatement. It has robbed me of my life. I wasn't even aware of what was going on for most of my life because I was too busy perfecting perfection.

Just to clarify, when I talk about perfectionism, I don't mean flowing hair, manicured fingernails, and an organized desk and bedroom. My life has pretty much always been a little chaotic and messy. My unopened bills are littered throughout my house in stacks tucked neatly under pillows and blankets. I usually pull my outfits out of a growing pile of clean clothes that are jammed in my laundry basket. They get re-routed to my bed to be put away, but at the end of the night, they get shoved back in the basket for a repeat performance tomorrow. Tomorrow, my favorite day of the year, where all my hopes, dreams and goals will be realized. Besides excelling in procrastination, I'm lazy and disheveled by nature. I have no problem leaving the house unshowered with yesterday's makeup still on. What can I say? I never got the picture-perfect girl memo that most of my female friends mastered flawlessly.

I'm talking about a deeper kind of perfectionism. The kind that has kept me from living fully. Stopping me in my tracks when my instinct says, "Do that thing you really want to do." Like speaking, singing, dancing, performing, expressing, feeling (yes, feeling), and all the other things I wanted to do naturally and creatively. But then I didn't because I felt I had to master it first—with 100% impeccability.

Perfectionism is an edit button on living.

I feel that I will be judged and hated if I'm myself, so I'll just be perfect—perfectly sweet and delightful. Roll with the flow, always be friendly and make others feel comfortable at all costs.

I was the sweet one. My sister was the rebel.

Or course, both and neither are true.

Looking back on my life, I have regrets. I wonder, "What would it all look like if I didn't give a damn?"

If only I had a small fraction of Madonna's balls. Or my sister's.

I used to love to sing. Music had always been my passion, my true happy place. I used to jump at every opportunity to sing. Whether it was in a choir, a performance group, or even just at vocal lessons, singing fueled my teenage dreams for stardom. Truthfully, I was probably average at best, but I didn't care because it was fun. I noticed how others were free with their voices. Like Madonna. It didn't matter that she wasn't the best singer. Her confidence was palpable, and I was mesmerized by it. I admired that quality. Whatever that was that allowed people to just be: I wanted that. They were the ones who would bust out a song at a party while someone played the guitar. Or someone would ask them.

"Wanna sing?" Or, "Hey, will you harmonize this?" Or, "Will you hop on stage and give this a try?"

They always said yes.

I was so fucking jealous of those people. Sometimes they weren't even that great (and annoyingly, sometimes they were), but they just went for it. I wanted to be like that. I wanted to be free, spontaneous, confident.

But I wasn't. There was no vocal confidence in me. I never felt good enough to get up and sing on a whim, and I only felt comfortable blending in a group. I figured I just needed to get this singing thing absolutely mastered before I could perform freely and own it. Like Madonna.

When I moved to Los Angeles, I decided I wanted to

become a professional "musical artist." I would work out all those pesky insecurities later. I kept up a very diligent regimen, and my goal of being good enough was always just out of reach. I went to singing lessons multiple times a week and would practice every single day, often for hours. That was pretty much the only consistent thing I did. Everything else in my life was a disaster. Practice, practice, practice. It was my only mission, and whatever fun I once had singing was long gone as I focused on making it big. I was always preparing for an opportunity that would happen sometime in the future.

Whenever I was asked, "What do you do?" I would respond proudly:

"I'm a singer."

Like clockwork, I would hear, "Oh, cool! Sing something?"

I had my response down. I would say I had a sore throat or a cough or cold. Some perfectly timed bullshit I came up with to throw people off asking me to simply "sing." Singers sing, right? Nope. Not me. I had to be perfect before I could ever sing in public. I wasn't going to embarrass myself until I was a better vocalist than Mariah Carey.

And that was never going to happen.

So there was no career.

I did do a bunch of things to keep the musician facade going. I performed in multiple shows, did cabaret in New York, and was in a couple of girl groups complete with a manager. I did lots of recordings and there were some people who really loved my voice. But not me. I didn't have confidence in myself. I would somehow pull through with massive amounts of anxiety, but I always felt that everyone else was better and that I needed to work harder to catch up. Of course, there are many singers out in the world raking in the millions with all kinds of voices, but I didn't think I was like them. So I just kept trying to "get there" instead of being myself. But I couldn't be myself. So I always found a way to self-sabotage or quit.

Maybe this wasn't the worst thing, since the joy I'd once felt while singing was long gone. The day I went from singing for fun to trying to "make it" was when I lost the entire point. My desire to be "perfect" and get it "right" meant that it was never, ever going to be good enough. I had completely missed the mark.

This scenario has played itself out in many different ways in my life. I have walked around completely self-obsessed and worried that at any moment someone might call on me to speak, give an opinion, or ask me to do something else for which I was not prepared. I was always on guard, always trying to be the best at whatever it was that I was doing. Walking around like an "I'm perfectly perfect" robot isn't realistic, and it presents a false image to the world. Who gives a damn if I sing off-key, or trip and fall while dancing, or stumble over my words in a speech? Those are the things that I admire in others. It's the flaws and the fuck-ups that pull me in and win me over, so why wouldn't that be the same for me? Isn't that the whole point of this crazy life anyway? Figuring it out as we go, picking ourselves up when we fall, and laughing along the way?

Life is a blip. Like a beautiful but tragic film that's over before you get settled. You try to replay it in your mind or even start it over, but when you do that, you're not being present, and meanwhile, time is passing and quickly. We're lucky if we get a do-over or a reframe, but often we don't, and the movie just ends without warning. For me, my playback is simple: I wish I hadn't taken myself so seriously and lost all those years trying to attain something just out of reach.

When I told my friend about my struggle with perfectionism, she offered me the most brilliant advice:

"Live in its opposite, in imperfection, and seek out opportunities where you can put yourself in situations where you're uncomfortably 'flawed.' Be messy. Get it wrong. Don't plan."

I've been given a lot of advice I didn't take, but for some reason I took hers. Which is strange because it was so casual, said over salad and cappuccino on Ventura Boulevard. I'd seen high-end therapists and various healers and spiritual teachers, desperately seeking answers, but that lunch on that particular day was when it clicked. I took her words to heart. Like, full-on. And then Brené Brown came on the scene, which gave me extra ammunition. It was like I was fully given permission to fail, and I was ready. I had no idea who Brené was when I discovered her, she was already well on her way to being a best-selling author many times over with books about perfectionism and more.

It was her TED Talk about shame that did it for me. She talked about how she wanted to break in and steal the video of her previous talk after she did it. She felt too exposed, too honest, too revealing and vulnerable. She had to get it back before anyone saw it. But how? Before she knew it, the video went viral and the rest is history. Her message hit me on a core level. My "perfectionism" was getting in the way of being myself. I was hiding.

Everything was coming together like little breadcrumbs—oddly, like the croutons in my salad.

First, it was speaking in groups without a plan, sharing my opinion, or just doing random things that I normally wouldn't do, like telling my secrets or writing about embarrassing things. I even took a stand-up comedy class and did a humiliating set. *What could be more terrifying than that?* I figured. What resulted was crazy: I started to feel really confident. Like a badass. I started feeling free. To the outside world, I probably looked emotional and borderline unstable (I was told this often), but inside I felt alive. It wasn't easy.

After any unusual exposure of "the real me," I would have what seemed like a catastrophic panic attack where I wanted to hide forever, but I would emerge, somehow, like an even wilder, more insane version of myself. However, the aftershock was nothing. What was the most challenging were the moments before "being me," that open window right before the act of courage. I saw how desperately I clung to safety and I would sob uncontrollably. I felt almost hysterical revealing myself. I was woken up in the night with a vicious voice screaming from within, "You can't do that." Warning me, at all costs, *NO! Do not seek freedom, it isn't going to work out for you.* It felt like the death of my perfect, safe self.

It was life-changing.

I'm not sure why it took me so long to figure this out. Some people never have to fight to just "be," but I don't have to envy them anymore because I know everyone has their own path. Madonna has her journey and I have mine. I wonder sometimes if I needed to hide myself in order to find myself. After I made my decision to be imperfect, I never went back to the old me, though I'm sure many wish that I would. Sweet is easier to handle.

But it isn't real. It isn't authentic and most people see the truth anyway. Like my sister.

The morning after our fight, she leaned in as she whispered:

"Don't worry, I know you're not perfect."

And we both fell over laughing. Maybe I hadn't been fooling anyone after all.

I DON'T LISTEN TO THE SMITHS
ANYMORE

ERIN RANTA

The week before my first day of high school, my mom started up her old, burgundy-colored Volvo without issue (which was always a pleasant surprise) and I flopped in the passenger seat beside her. We pulled into the parking lot of our neighborhood drug store and I hopped out of the car, on a mission to arm myself with the coolest school supplies: pink plastic boxes for my pens and pencils, Lisa Frank-designed everything and gel pens in every color.

As I scoured the shelves, a melody caught my attention and my senses shifted away from the smell of the erasers to the music coming through the speakers. *Dun, da-da-da dun, dun, dee doo, daaaa...dun, da-da-da dun, dun, dee, doo, daaaa...*it was the opening of Tchaikovsky's "The Nutcracker." As the tune continued, my thoughts of school supplies faded and my body stirred, remembering the moves from my childhood roles in the Pacific Northwest Ballet's production of the classic ballet. It had been two years since I'd done any sort of ballet, and I was moved to tears from the auditory memory.

Soon after that day, I rejoined ballet classes, attending six days a week. It was the drug I looked forward to after what was usually a shitty, anxiety-filled day of feeling invisible at school. I knew for at least 90 minutes I would be with my only two best friends: music and movement. Now that my body had grown from 4'2" to 5'3", after a bout with thyroid disease, kids had stopped asking me, "How's the weather down there?" Boys were starting to glance my way, and I could feel the obsession with looking perfect—quite a strong force. Every 90 minutes of ballet class were a chance to perfect my physical body, and to reconnect with my emotions in the process.

Nearly every day, I hurried across Capitol Hill into the warmth of that studio's changing room, where I would yank on my pink mesh-seamed tights with the feet cut out. Over that, I donned my burgundy tank with the low back and my Mirabella brand leotard, which was cut at the bottom like a pair of boy shorts. I always tried to keep my shirt pulled down over my butt as I transferred from underwear to tights and leotard. Finally, I adjusted my feet into my canvas split sole ballet slippers, with the elastics forming an "X" on top of each foot.

The two-sink counter in the changing room was always crowded with dancers getting ready for class, but I would still squish in to strategically tuck about 15 bobby pins around my bun, slipping a medium brown Goodie hairnet around it and folding it over twice. After that, I removed whatever CD was in my large Discman (which was usually Nirvana's *Nevermind,* the Notorious B.I.G.'s "Juicy" or "Big Poppa" from *Ready to Die* or something by Tupac), wrapping my headphones tightly around its white and orange casing and securing it in my bag.

Once I locked my book bag in a locker, I raced into the assigned studio to reserve my favorite spot at the barre. There were barres secured to the wall, but I always chose the one in the center because DG, the accompanist, could see me from there (and on my good side). His music made me feel otherworldly, as if I had a secret power.

Being an accomplished Seattle musician active in the arts

scene, he knew a good dancer when he saw one, and he told me I was good, that I had talent. I had a penchant for adagio and slow, gushy movements, he would say. I was not some quick, petite allegro girl; I loved the melodramatic, gorgeous, lyrical, dark music. His words always made me swell with pride.

The instructor would explain the combination quickly before the music began. During the five, six, seven, eight intro, I would shift into the most emotional mood I could muster and dance my fucking soul out—particularly during ronds de jambe and adagios.

I felt like moving to music was all I had.

After class, I kept on the sweaty tights and leotard and put on my dark gray sweatshirt and Levi's. I'd found the jeans at a second-hand store and thought they were so cool because they had a purple paisley knee patch sewn over a hole in the knee. Lastly, I put on my brown Doc Martens.

The sweat on my skin often gave me chills at the bus stop, but I loved it. Though I could have stood and listened to my Discman while waiting for the #7, I usually set my backpack on the sidewalk and reenacted adagio combinations from class as best I could instead. On the corner of Broadway and Roy, right in front of Siam Thai, I floated my arms overhead and raised my legs as high as my jeans would allow. After the #7 came, I would transfer to the #30, which took me back to the outskirts of Laurelhurst, our affluent neighborhood that felt worlds away from the excitement and escape of downtown Seattle.

I wanted to hold onto my escape as long as I could and cherished the long bus ride.

Once I returned home, I never knew what to expect. The seeds of divorce had been planted, yet my parents were still living in the same house.

"Your mother is out again, and she left the house a mess," my Dad would mutter under his breath. I later recognized his behavior as passive-aggressive, but at the time, I was confused, hurt, and wanted to block it out. I untangled the headphones (no matter how neatly I wrapped them, they would always get knotted up), checked which earbud had the *L,* and inserted it in my left ear, the other in my right.

To add to the uncomfortable tension at home, I had this damn thyroid disorder, which had stunted my growth so severely for so long that I actually started saving up allowance money for a bone-stretching procedure I saw an advertisement for on television. Thankfully, my thyroid medicine worked and I did start growing in height, at least looking more normal on the outside.

In childhood, dance was my first escape; in high school, drinking was my second. By the time I got to college, my life revolved around both.

At the University of Washington, I majored in modern dance —the kind where you rolled around on the floor, sometimes in a heap of bodies, but also used your breath and core to ignite movement. I was learning about finding an artistic voice, about choreography, contact improvisation, and the liberation of a woman chopping off her hair. At the same time, I was stuck living in a sorority with girls who lived to make colorful banners for the neighboring frat house, matching them with ribbons wrapped around their long, blonde ponytails that hung down to their ankle socks.

I sought solace in finding (since I was still underage) and drinking as much alcohol as I could, and in the composer Philip Glass—his Violin Concerto No. 2, to be exact. It was eight-and-a-half minutes of pulsating violins and mournful motifs running rampant, cycling through drama, beauty, power, and sadness with a gorgeous culmination at the end. It was a beautiful piece that escalated the way I wished my life would.

Every night, drinking or not, I played that piece on my Discman while I lay in bed, mentally choreographing various routines. On every walk home from dance class to my sorority, I would listen and try to process my emptiness. In the coming years, my life's most pronounced escalation was my move from habitual drug and alcohol use into full-fledged addiction.

I had sensed even towards the end of high school that drinking was becoming a problem when I would skip ballet to go do it. All the while, I held onto songs from The Smiths, Nick Cave, Beethoven, Kate Bush, the Kronos Quartet, and Philip Glass for dear life as I navigated my double life as an addict and dancer turned Pilates instructor.

I tried to keep my obsessions with drinking and dancing parallel and in balance for as many years as I could. When I eventually stopped dancing and could not crank out triple pirouettes anymore, the music remained. Instead of finding it in dance, music was its own solace.

Somewhat symbolically, music took on an abrupt new role in my life one day. Having quit drinking, I had been busy building my now-sober life, finding things to look forward to that did not involve alcohol or drugs and working on rebuilding my strength. One spring afternoon four years into my sobriety, while pregnant and walking in New York City to the subway, I pulled out my phone and put my earbuds in each ear, again looking for the imprinted letter *L* to verify which ear was which. I opened Spotify, looking for something to listen to on my trek from Queens to the Upper West Side.

As I pulled up the app, I drew a blank. My yearning for the raspy sounds of Tom Waits was gone. My hankering for Guns N' Roses' "Don't Cry" and "November Rain," ballads which had made me cry in the past, was nonexistent. It hit me: I no longer needed my dark, slow, sad music. I no longer needed to escape.

"There Is a Light That Never Goes Out" by The Smiths is a song that I will cherish forever, as it carried me through many anxiety-ridden hangovers. My eyes do not well up with tears when I hear it anymore, however, nor do I even search for the song.

My sobriety, my health, and my baby helped me segue from always choosing the ballad to now choosing songs that were up-tempo. Though my reverence and appreciation for the adagio will live forever, I can now listen from outside the dark, sad place I used to live.

After being stumped for a moment on that New York spring day, I put on some Beyoncé and walked from Columbus Circle to 72nd and Broadway and smiled thinking about how a song could be just that: a song.

REBUILDING THE DREAM

AMY LIZ HARRISON

The ethereal Carrara marble bar top was housed by a tall mahogany structure in my new dining room. I'd never lived in a house with such an ostentatious bar before, and I certainly didn't expect to find one in what was soon to be our young family's new home. The aches of my insecurities and inadequacies were quieted as I began to dream about the life of fulfillment I aspired to find in this space: the classy high society parties I planned to host would be the bridge to the intimate friendships I hoped to develop. I was enamored by the endless possibilities and the Gatsby-esque magic of the romantic space that was surely going to be the ticket to my social upgrade.

I unpacked boxes, painted walls, and arranged the furniture. Building the house into a home, I imagined, required turning that bar into an inviting space. I purchased beautiful martini glasses, LED lighting for the liquor bottle shelves, elegant long-stemmed wine glasses, and old crystal highballs. The wine bottles were categorized, proudly displaying their colorful and artistic labels; reds were carefully placed on temperature-controlled racks, whites rested politely in the chiller fridge.

Eventually, crowding around that bar surrounded by the beaming, wine-stained smiles of my "friend-quaintances" became a routine. Wine in hand, idle conversation and delightfully inappropriate jokes rolled off their tongues. The volume of our laughter increased steadily, right alongside our rising blood alcohol levels, as the evening progressed.

I felt warm, connected and integrated by way of the consumption of liquid lubricant. For those fleeting hours, I felt whole. Looking around at the ever increasing exuberance and inebriation of the cohort, I was convinced: *I was living the dream.* My eyes were transfixed on my newfound companions' glasses as they emptied them, determined not to let them run dry. I wielded a bottle, constant refills at the ready—as if keeping their glasses full would somehow ensure my associates' continued presence and loyalty in my life.

Carefully, I constructed a rickety house of cards disguised as a fulfilling life, but just one gust of wind would prove it was a façade. I had built a toilet-paper-thin fantasy world of faux connections masquerading as true friendships. The bar and its bottles became my world, my desperate and futile quest to find emotional satisfaction and mental peace. Ever chasing the optimistic idea that someday, I'd feel satiated.

Over time, I collected some of the typical trophies of the drunks as if I were checking off boxes on a scorecard: Impression management. The constant pursuit of protecting my delicate house of cards from any draft. Assorted physical Injuries. Broken promises. Bloated face. Humiliated children. Mockery of sacred events. Shattered dreams. Glassy eyes staring back at me in the mirror. Ruined relationships. Multiple bumpers annihilated on a long list of vehicles. The constant tired appearance of someone who rarely slept. Pounding headaches.

Then came that proverbial gust of wind. Like a nightmare I couldn't wake up from, there was the memory of the red and blue police lights. There was the walk of shame. The wobbly, one-footed, outstretched-arm sobriety test on the main artery through town. The neighbor driving off with my kids as I was placed in the backseat of a police car. After an emotionally excruciating night in jail, my soul was shattered by the reality of my actions. I limped through the doors of rehab raw, broken, and dejected.

Much like demolition work on an old ramshackle fixer-upper, rehab crumbled my walls, revealing the hidden and rotting parts of me that had corroded the entire infrastructure. I had to surrender to the process of being razed to the ground. My next task would be to painstakingly build the new framework on an alcohol-free journey and then reconstruct myself—one rough and grainy brick at a time.

Begrudgingly at first, I knew it was time to assimilate to my new bar-less and booze free life at home. Still nicked and bruised from handling the shrapnel of my old life, I prepared to emerge from the protective walls of treatment, hoping I wouldn't fall back into the rubble of addiction.

When I stepped over the threshold and into my house, a chill ran down my spine. I was a stranger in my own home. The walls were recognizable, but I was not the same person. Muscle memory magnetized my body to the bar. It was empty.

The mahogany shelving for liquor and glasses had been taken down. Someone had spackled and painted over the nail holes where the LED lighting used to be as if it had never existed in the first place. Almost as if *I* had never existed.

I stretched my shaky hands out and placed them tentatively on the cold marble bar top, now totally empty. A wave of sorrow washed over me. I swallowed hard a few times, attempting to eliminate the cottony feeling in my throat.

"My life is over," I whispered as tears welled in my eyes.

What I didn't realize was that *my life was actually just beginning* —I just had to stay the course and continue reforming.

Initially despondent, I decided to try to pursue a sober life, even though I felt unstable and uncertain. After all, I had nothing to lose and possibly everything to gain. Letting fear be my fuel, I followed the recommendations passed on to me in treatment. I began going to meetings, procured a sponsor, and became accustomed to calling other 12-Step members when I felt uncomfortable in my skin. Gradually, I realized taking direction was helping me assemble a solid foundation.

The key to my sobriety was following the blueprints exactly as they were laid out for me. Creating new habits. Fostering new friendships. Foraging new activities to build my life around. Eventually, I discovered I was no longer in constant crisis and chaos. I was moving from struggle to safety.

By the time two years had passed, I was situated at another piece of furniture made of mahogany. This time, I was sitting at a conference table in a leather chair. Flipping through page after page, pens in hand, my husband and I signed the purchase papers on a new home. Upon completion of the cornucopia of signatures, my husband turned to face me.

"You've earned this new house," he whispered. "This new life." I gulped and shook my head, thinking of the nights he spent picking me up from dive bars and the mornings he spent bringing me coffee, attempting to restore me to life after another inebriated adventure.

"*We've* earned this new house and this new life," I corrected him as we interlaced our hands together on the shiny tabletop.

Selling the house was like writing a check that my heart couldn't cash. Packing day arrived and I tried to remain task-oriented, hoping my bittersweet feelings would dissipate as I traveled through each room of the house where we had spent a decade raising kids. I dug a path through a sea of cardboard moving boxes and bubble wrap, brandishing a marker in my right hand and a roll of packing tape in my left. *Kitchen. Downstairs Powder Room. Guest Room.* I scrawled in squeaky sharpie as I labeled each box.

Slowly, I navigated the house where we'd built so much life. Room by room, I recalled an array of memories from across the spectrum from excitement and elation to melancholy and despair. There was the wood kitchen floor where one of my daughters took her first wobbly steps. The marshmallow-puffed living room couch where I had passed out countless times in a drunken stupor. The bunkbeds in my sons' room where I relentlessly tickled them, causing their little toddler bodies to thrash and jerk as they exploded in giggles. The doorway I'd walked through when I welcomed my newborn babies home from the hospital. The guest room where I came to, blurry-eyed and confused after a blackout. The master bathroom where we discovered, through tears, double lines on a pregnancy test, indicating the impending arrival of an unexpected blessing.

My heart still glowing from reliving specters and milestones from the past, I descended the staircase and stopped abruptly. My eyes had fallen upon the old fair-weather friend I'd largely ignored for some time now: the empty and lifeless mahogany bar. I caught my reflection in the mirror, still hanging adjacent to where I'd spent so much time drinking just a couple of short years ago. I noticed my eyes were clear, my face no longer puffy and bloated. I looked well rested.

Placing the marker between my teeth and the tape on my wrist, I meandered over the erect and commanding structure. I stretched my now steady hands out and watched them move with purpose through the air, landing on the bar. The marble slab felt unwelcoming and frigid. Closing my eyes for a moment, I was curious to see if this bar still held dominion over me. I tried to reconnect to my old dream and the wine-stained smiles of old friends, but those once-vivid memories were already sparse and fading. I cocked my head to one side, listening for the old sounds of drunken merriment. Nothing. The silence was comforting. It sounded like peace.

I snapped out of my musings to the *clip-clop* sound of high-heeled shoes out on the driveway. The doorbell rang. Before I had the chance to invite her in, my realtor opened the front door and popped her mop of curly, chocolate colored bobbed hair inside.

"Knock, knock!" she called out as she shuffled across the foyer on her patent leather beige Natrualizer pumps, a cloud of

White Shoulders perfume following her every step. She waved a keychain in the air, which jingle-jangled in sync with the movement of her wrist. "Con-grat-u-la-tions!" She said in a sing-song voice with staccato syllabled. She dropped the keychain onto the ghostly glowing marble bar top with a clink. Attached to the keychain was a shiny brass key, the key to our new house.

Time to go.

My new start in my new home, courtesy of my new life in recovery, was waiting for me. I felt so drastically different from my former self who had become enslaved to the bar. No longer did I feel drawn to it, utterly powerless over my molasses-thick addiction. I no longer suffered from an acute broken spirit, desperately scrambling to find clarity and movement in my paralyzing and blinding fog of constant shame. What weightless joy to realize there was nothing I needed from the bar area anymore. After all, I was the one who had attached meaning to it anyway.

The following morning, the movers fired up the diesel moving trucks and inched out of the neighborhood. My family was waiting for me in the suburban mom-mobile, gently idling in the driveway. I was ready too. Nothing remained for me to attend to within those four walls.

I sauntered out of the now-empty house with its old memories and stepped into the light. Facing forward, I reached back around my hip to grasp the doorknob. I pulled the door shut behind me without looking back. Taking a deliciously deep breath, I threw my head back and closed my eyes, letting the warm glow of the sun fall gently on my face. Enveloped in the liberation of my lucid life, I felt almost intoxicated by the serenity of my sobriety.

At once, I realized: *everything I had been searching for in that robust bar was paradoxically found in its absence.* Honesty about my insecurities had evolved into true connection with humans. The hope of becoming a socialite had melted as I discovered the joy of serving others. Sowing the seeds of positive action had been the catalyst to metamorphosing into a woman with self-esteem who didn't hide her inadequacies. Emotional and mental chaos were replaced by a calm, docile inner satisfaction. This was freedom. *I was living the dream.*

The rest was just marble, wood, glass, labels, and varnish.

GOING FROM IMPORTANT TO WHAT WAS REALLY IMPORTANT

TIMOTHY GAGER

W hat I used to think was important:

Number of drinks.
Number of women.
Loyalty.
Unconditional friendships.

All four of these were in play and measuring my value from the time I started drinking to about ten years ago. I hosted a "very important" event, The Dire Literary Series. The series, held in an art gallery, had been described in a Boston newspaper as a party in your living room with drinks—though there also just so happened to be a literary reading involved. At series events, we liked to keep the party going, since life as I knew it was just that: a party.

On one night's event in particular, which featured Victor David Giron, Michael Atwood, and Leo Racicot, I announced we would be walking up the street to The People's Republik for drinks. I needed the "we" to be around people that night as I did most every night, so there was no need to change it—no need to change anything, ever.

The last time I thought something needed to change was in 1985. I made a call to the Delaware General Service Assembly of Alcoholics Anonymous. I needed a second opinion about my feelings about alcohol and I needed some help immediately, though maybe not in sequential order—I needed both right that second! Usually, my solution to having feelings was a drink or a few lines of cocaine, as nothing worked nearly as fast. I didn't know what I needed, but a phone hotline, as I saw it, was for desperate people who needed to be spoken off the ledge. And that was where I stood, with a troubled wind roaring and me about to be blown off. Ironically, that summer, I had worked a suicide hotline and was scared to death the entire time that someone might call. I never received a single phone call the entire summer, which was good, because I was high most of the time. Now, I was making my own call to Alcoholics Anonymous, and they were saying they would call me back.

Call me back? It wasn't the immediate fix I wanted, and my favorite bar was right up the street (see under what is important: *number of drinks*). To give credit where it was due, they did call me back. The only issue was I was out at the bar. When I arrived home, my roommate tried to tell me that I had a message, but I cut him off.

"Wrong number!" I barked at him. I retreated into my room, and that was the end of that.

I turn back the clock a lot. *What If?* is a game I play frequently, a game about regret. *What if* I had completed my original major in college? *What if* I hadn't overslept the day of my GMAT? *What if* I didn't handle people, places and things like an asshole? An alternative name for it is *I Meant to Do That!* It's part of the same game, but here I get to justify my consequences without having faults or admitting mistakes—I can quickly show you how it's played.

Eleven months before that night at The People's Republik, I was dating a person named Laurie, a woman six years sober (see under what is important: *number of women*). I used Laurie to fill the vacant hole in my life. I told her I was a social drinker. This was a good lie because if I told the truth, I already knew that as a woman six years into recovery, Laurie would not want any relationship with me (again, see under what is important: *number of women*). At the time, I would tell any lie to mislead people about my drinking if it worked to my advantage.

Saturday dates with Laurie ended at 4 pm because she had an AA meeting to go to.

"No problem, do what you need to do," I would tell her. When she wasn't around, what I needed to do was drink. Laurie was already on to me after we traveled to a party in upstate New York and I fell asleep there under the pool table. It seemed like a good solution for lodging at the time, as I had not booked a hotel.

At the time, my best friend Katrina and I used to drink almost every day. She was loyal (see under what is important: *loyalty*). She put up with nearly all of my bullshit and remained my friend (see under what is important: *unconditional friendships*). Laurie's cautiousness quickly changed into avoidance when I posted pictures on Facebook of Katrina and I driving back from Rhode Island with drinks in our hands. I was in a blackout and I was driving. I didn't give a shit about drinking and driving or posting pictures on Facebook for all to see. My relationship with sober Laurie was officially over. *I meant to do that!*

Now, back to coming out of a blackout at The People's Republik 11 months later.

I came out of it in a full-blown conversation with someone I had never met before. He was my usual type of new friend: young-ish, red-faced and gin-blossomed. I knew Chris, the person sitting behind him, as an artist and a piss-in-his-pants drinker who had been told he had to stop drinking or he would die. The people I had come with, one of which was Katrina, were no longer there. This was not a good sign.

I tried to call Katrina, but it went straight to voicemail. I knew I had either said or done something horrible, which was why I was alone with Chris and my new slurring buddy. Scenes such as these had played out before—not just people leaving me at bars, but people leaving my life entirely.

Leaving The People's Republik that night, I was woeful and devastated. I knew the alcohol was making me feel worse, but I couldn't shake the feeling of abandonment. I made 15 more calls to Katrina and again, all 15 went straight to voicemail.

It was freezing and I was walking the streets of Cambridge, Massachusetts, trying to find my car with no one to help me. Ironically, I found Katrina's car and concluded that she and the people she drove with must be still out in Cambridge, wanting no part of me. I returned to the same parking lot a few times in my search, as if my car or even Katrina would magically appear, but neither of them did.

I then remembered a trick I had learned as the Designated Person Picked to Drive. This was a title I used that was similar to Designated Driver, but it meant the person who was most likely still able to drive despite still having drank. The trick was pressing the remote on a key chain until you heard your car's horn or saw its headlights flash. Finally, after another half-hour doing this, I saw a flash of light and heard my car horn beep.

Walking around had sobered me up somewhat, but it had also put me in the bad bubble of not feeling drunk but not being able to pass a breathalyzer. Still, it was better than driving in a blackout, which was something that had started to happen a lot; more than a few times, I'd called people on my way home in that state. The next day they would call to see if I was okay because I hadn't sounded well on the phone and had entered the I-93 North ramp going the wrong way. They would tell me they were worried about me, but no one would tell me to stop drinking. No one would dare.

As I drove home from The People's Republik after all this, I again serial-dialed the people I came with, leaving voice messages ranging from apologetic to morose to angry. In some of them, I was downright attempting stand-up comedy. Being bipolar was not one of my diagnoses at the time, but if those voice messages were ever released, that diagnosis would not have been unreasonable.

By the time I got home, I realized a few things. First, I had no friends; second, I could not stop drinking; third, I often drove after drinking, even if I was loaded. If I forced myself to think about these things, it would also force me to admit that I needed help, which I was not willing to do.

I also couldn't sleep. I didn't want to sleep—I just wanted to feel sorry for myself, which also happened often. Sometimes, in order to sleep, I counted methods of committing suicide, which is a dystopian version of counting sheep. Then the next morning, I had to motivate myself to do something—anything—so my brain didn't stay in that depressed state. I was always pretty good at picking myself up by my bootstraps; it's what I thought being a "self-starter" meant.

By daybreak, I had moved from the floor to the sofa, still thinking about my friends who wanted nothing to do with me. My friends from last night were now my ex-friends. I was tired of this happening over and over again, and I felt like I was immersed in the pain of every broken heart in the universe.

I thought about my last relationship, the one with Laurie 11 months before, and how dishonest I'd been. I must have caused her so much pain as well. Why did I think that living in this much pain was just a part of normal life?

Suddenly, I remembered that it was Saturday. When we were dating, Laurie used to leave my house on Saturdays to go to her recovery meeting, which was only 10 minutes away—and today, was still nine hours or so from starting. I stayed on the sofa as time ticked by slowly. I turned on the television, uninterested in anything that was on.

I had spent all morning and afternoon concluding I needed everything to change if I wanted something better for myself.

Until that day, I had spent my entire life not knowing that I had to change everything. All of the things I listed in my head that I felt were so important really never were. Finally, it was late afternoon and time to get in my car to get to the only meeting I knew existed.

I AM THE COMMON DENOMINATOR IN MY LIFE

JEANNE FOOT

My mother reminded me how I was such a "lucky girl" who should be grateful. I felt like she was talking about someone else. My external world appeared charmed, as if I had it all. It was true that I didn't want for much, but emotionally, I fell prey to severe neglect. Material needs didn't mean anything to me, as my soul more than paid the price for what I experienced. But my parents couldn't see that my pain was excruciating.

I was born and raised in the early '60s in London, England, to a loving middle-class family in an era where the adage "children should be seen and not heard" was the norm. As a child, I quickly learned that feelings were discouraged. I was often dismissed as being "too sensitive" or "overly emotional," forcing me to put up a façade that everything was okay, setting me up for a lifetime of conforming to others' expectations. Emotions were feared as weakness rather than normal human responses, most brilliantly demonstrated by my parents on October 3, 1963, when I was four years old.

A policeman walked into my house, but I was not scared because he was extremely kind to me. He helped me get dressed and gave me breakfast. I knew something was amiss because the policeman wanted to drive me to school. As we pulled up right in front, I could see my friends looking at me inside the car with POLICE written on the outside and the shiny red siren on top. With everyone watching, I felt something stir inside me that I had never felt before, which made me feel incredibly special and important. Little did I know I would learn to chase that feeling for my life.

The unexplained loss and grief the day my baby sister died lived with me for decades. My parents never explained to me what happened to Rachel, but I figured it out and sensed it was a defining moment in my life. It would be years before I would be able to make peace with her passing. As I grew older, so did the magnitude of the loss. I mourned the potential of *what she could have been* had she lived as my lifelong sister. This tragedy was compounded by my parents never mentioning her name again.

My remaining sibling was my brother, Wayne, who was six years older, two feet taller, and an intravenous heroin user who babysat me when my parents went out. Our relationship was incredibly volatile. I felt as if I was trying to dodge the bullets of his manic craziness, sandwiched between his occasional bouts of kindness. Eventually, I fell victim to the most unspeakable acts any child should have to endure, leaving me vulnerable. I had to fend for myself.

Saying no was as tricky as saying yes. Either way, I feared the backlash of "not being cooperative." To keep some semblance of my life being predictable, I would either befriend him or go to great lengths to avoid him as I orchestrated every move of mine to avoid colliding with him.

In retrospect, many moments from childhood seemed like they belonged in an action-packed, blockbuster movie. Police cars and ambulances regularly showed up at our house. Walking home from school, I often peered around corners to see what awaited me. On bad days, I asked my best friend if I could go to her house instead. We never spoke about what was going on at my house as I think she knew how embarrassed it made me, but she always welcomed me to her own.

Growing up, I had a penchant for chaos. It was familiar to me. Combined with my sharp intellect, chaos was my survival mode. I was a chameleon who managed to blend in and yet not draw too much attention to myself to keep danger at bay. My behavior was high-risk, and being a high-functioning party girl required a certain kind of tenacity.

My hatred for myself ran deep. I berated myself constantly about how flawed I was, and the shame was relentless. It followed me around like a younger sibling, wanting to hang out. My inner critic hurled highlight reels at me, displaying all that I'd done wrong rather than what I had done right. I started to think of taking my life as the incessant chatter was driving me to the brink, and I knew this wasn't sustainable. My logic was to counter those feelings with anything that would make them go away. To not feel was paramount because nothing could prevent me from the only thing I knew would make me feel better: not feeling anything.

Over the years, our family problems became very public. My brother had a knack for ending up on the front page of the newspaper. In one of his darkest moments, he robbed seven banks with a dog and ended up on the news as the "doggy bandit" and eventually did time in a maximum-security prison.

As adults, my husband and I would visit him with my parents on Visitor's Day, accompanying them for moral support. The car ride there was long, and I let my eyes drift out the window, lost in the miles of green fields as I listened to my parents argue about what the next best move was to reverse the mess he had gotten himself into.

Wayne would pressure me to sneak drugs into the jail on Visitor's Day because drugs were worth more inside than cash. When I refused, he would have a violent outburst, cursing and swearing at me: "What kind of f**king sister are you?" I second-guessed myself, like a battered woman wondering if I should have said yes.

From the time I was a teenager right up until I was a young adult, I used my "trauma" as a pass to excuse all my behavior. How I saw it was I behaved the way I did because anyone would do the same if they were in my shoes. I was street-smart, defensive, and argumentative. I saw myself as a victim with rights.

My entire life, I felt my parents misunderstood me. Their preoccupation was with my older brother who was a time bomb waiting to explode; as such, they were blind to the reality of my life.

I had tried to approach my parents about what had happened in my formative years when my brother used to babysit me and earned a textbook response from my parents: "Are you telling the truth?" I thought they had to be kidding—how could they not see that Wayne had taken the whole family hostage? They were in denial, which has been the problem all along. This should not have surprised me, yet it did. My parents were never able to agree as to the right way forward with Wayne.

I had a front-row seat and sometimes a starring role in the nightmare that impacted every fiber of my being. Our family lived by the "stiff upper lip" mentality of not speaking out about things, and I had broken that cardinal rule by confirming that my experiences existed.

Dread was a constant companion of mine, and I was always waiting for something to go wrong. Invariably, I was right; something always happened, like in October 1989. It was a Friday night and my husband and I were on our way downtown to my parents' place with our two young sons for Shabbat dinner, a weekly family ritual that divides one week from the next. As we settled in to enjoy the evening, there was a knock at the door, and my dad called out to me to answer it. I was shocked to see a police officer standing there, asking to speak to my parents. As my father approached the door, I knew something was "wrong," but could never have guessed the magnitude of the situation until the words rolled out of his mouth.

"Are you the parents of Wayne X?" the officer asked my father.

"Yes," he responded.

"I have some news for you," the officer said. "We've found your son's body and his emergency contacts; his parents were on his passport." I heard a gasp come out of my dad's mouth. The sound was as if all the air had expired from him as he ushered the policeman into the house.

I could never have anticipated how Wayne's death would charter me into unknown territory. The way I had navigated my life was always in a calculated manner, being at least a few steps ahead of him to preempt any danger or crisis. With this realization, I was able to take my first deep breath and inhale deeply into my lungs. I intuitively knew that the moment was much more significant than I could fully comprehend.

I remember the moment of clarity once he was gone, never to return. I received this from my Source: *He can't come after me anymore. He can't hurt me. I don't have to hide because he's gone, and I'm finally free.*

The magnitude of that realization took time to fully sink in. It started with an eerie silence, during which various scenes of his abuse flashed through my head. Afterwards, I was awash in a newfound freedom I had never experienced—it was akin to someone held hostage for years suddenly being set free, in a daze and unsure how it could be true.

Years later, we went to therapy as a family for grief counseling. In time, it came out that my brother was not a loving, caring brother, and the truth of who he really was emerged.

I sat on the couch in my therapist's office, just a few feet away from my mother. I could not stop fidgeting; my knee was pumping up and down like a piston as I waited for the next round of questions. I pretended to be interested in the art on the walls to ignore the silence, each second feeling like an eternity when it suddenly crescendoed:

"How do you show your daughter that you love her?" I heard my therapist ask my mother. *Go, team therapist*, I thought. Now we were onto something.

My mother looked as glamorous as she always did. She wore a long skirt (as she did not own even one pair of pants), killer boots, jewelry that declared she was someone who had everything and a hat that only the "royals" would wear, with her flaming red hair flowing out from beneath it.

"Oh, you know us English people," I heard her answer. "We are not the touchy-feely type."

All the memories of my childhood came flooding in. My mother's criticism had been like a mantra on repeat, asking: *What's wrong with you?* My father's voice in my head played the other mantra I had grown accustomed to: *Pull yourself together.* As I silently tried to keep my composure, she continued: "This is how we English people feel: we just don't."

I was stunned by her lack of sensitivity towards me. Did she not stop to wonder how it felt to hear what she had just said? So how did she show her love, then? I wanted to know because I was beginning to believe that maybe something really *was* wrong with me.

I moved to the chair to create some distance from my mother. She seemed so unnatural to me at times. As someone always looking for a back door or an escape, my first inclination was to get up and run.

I looked over at my mother to see what was coming next. It was clear how different we were, how much I needed to define myself as her opposite. In that damn therapist's office, she stood for what things *looked* like while I was a crusader for justice.

Wayne's death became the catalyst of the most authentic and genuine version of me 2.0. It unleashed a flood of emotions that I had buried for decades. I knew intrinsically that I was barely hanging on and I had to change my ways. I was not "using" like "others," as the people around me seemed to be able to stop without difficulty or least knew when they had enough. I had tried many times to stop the cycle, but not without great difficulty. Sunday nights eventually became Friday nights until my husband confronted me, and I told myself I had to get it together. Losing my children was non-negotiable for me, and I knew they deserved better. I loved my children more than myself, so I made an unwavering commitment to transmute my adversity. I knew that unless I consciously chose to embrace my unique soul's purpose in the school of Earth, I would keep repeating the same patterns I had learned from childhood.

I channeled my tenacious spirit into my recovery, which sent me on a quest to heal from my formative years. I chose a pathway of sobriety. Although it wasn't my first choice, it was the path I knew I had to walk. It took decades of self-inquiry and therapists of all kinds to slowly thaw my emotions out and allow me to see a clearer picture of what life was about.

I was hungry for change. I consumed everything that was related to spirituality, addiction, trauma, and mental health. I even went as far as shamanism, kundalini yoga, neuroscience, behavioral change, and personal transformation. I went back to school and studied to become a therapist, and I continue to invest in my own healing both as a student and a teacher of somatic modalities and holistic recovery.

Throughout this 30-year journey, my heart has become wholehearted and healed. I have increased my capacity to give and receive love, and I am working on increasing my joy quota daily. I have grown to know over time that all of me is welcome here, that I am loved no matter what has happened to me. My lived experience has led me to make peace with my history and create a new story, one with authenticity, vulnerability, and compassion for all.

I recognized that regardless of my history, it was my responsibility to create the changes in my life. I made a vow: *This stops this generation, now.* Change happened for me when I realized it was I who was the common thread in my life. Because no matter where I go, I am there. I was ready to accept that I was the common denominator.

When I think back to the feisty young girl who dragged her mother to her therapist's office seeking validation for what she had experienced, I realize I could never have anticipated the process of lifelong self-inquiry that would follow. I'm grateful that the young girl's willingness to be curious, unlearn, and relearn would eventually connect her heart and head.

A LONG WALK BACK FROM AUSTRALIA

SUELEN ROMANI

"I can't make this decision for you," my therapist Lisa said. "Maybe you should wait a little longer before you travel with him. Keep focused on your recovery."

I'd been sober for nine months after a bad relapse on my 32nd birthday that left me feeling like death was looming over my shoulder. The abstinence afterward was physical hell and none of my previous coping mechanisms were working, so I called my mother. She'd helped me find Lisa.

Early in therapy, Lisa directed me in taking two actions: going to AA meetings and finding a job. My first AA group was at the Rainbow Bar and Grill on Sunset Boulevard, a small dark room where people gathered every weekday at noon to learn to live sober. My first work in sobriety was at Mel's Diner, also on Sunset. I worked the 11 pm to 7 am shift. The nights were busy, as the diner was one of LA's after-party food spots.

Lisa also suggested that I avoid getting emotionally involved with anyone, especially early in sobriety, but it was too late. I had fallen in love with Tyler.

We'd met during a concert an old friend invited me to at Bar Sinister in Hollywood. Tyler had been playing keyboards and throughout the entire concert, he stared at me constantly. He moved to the sound of the music, sliding his hands on the keys like it was the easiest thing in the world; meanwhile, he smiled every time my eyes met his. It seemed like he was playing for me. While I was flattered, I was also uncomfortable with the intensity of his attention.

When the show was over, I met my friend backstage and we were introduced. Initially, I thought he wasn't my type. He was too skinny, and I preferred more athletic types. He was talented, but he looked scrawny. I gave him my number anyway, and he called almost every day, inviting me to his gigs even though I wasn't interested. One night he was playing at The Roxy, a venue I enjoyed, so I decided to join him. After his show that night, we went to his studio in Glendale. He showed me his music and I showed him some of my favorite Brazilian artists. Then, he gently rested his hand on the back of my neck and we kissed.

That was it. I was hooked.

Soon after we started hanging out, I traveled with him to a concert he was playing in Las Vegas. It was Labor Day weekend and the city was busy with pool parties everywhere. That weekend, I relapsed with a glass of sauvignon blanc, even though I'd been sober for three years. I also found out Tyler had a girlfriend in Australia who called him every hour to find out what he was doing. I hated that, that he was a cheater, but I didn't expect our little summer romance to last. I also didn't expect my glass of wine would send me so far downhill so fast.

It took me 28 days to hit bottom again, which happened on my birthday. Tyler and I had kept in touch and that weekend, he was on tour in Australia. He called daily to tell me that he missed me and LA and about how his girlfriend made his life difficult, but he couldn't leave her. Sometimes he'd lie; other times, he'd get angry. At first, I didn't care. I was on a drinking binge that was rapidly progressing.

After my birthday's drug and alcohol extravaganza, I knew I had to change again. Within a few days, I found Lisa, started working a 12-step program and got a sponsor. I was committed to turning my life around.

"I'm not drinking anymore," I said to Tyler on one of our calls. "I'm sober now and that's how I plan to stay."

"Good on you, babe. Good on you," he answered, laughing.

Tyler had a strong Australian accent that I enjoyed imitating. We had a lot of fun together over the phone. By the time he arrived back in Los Angeles, I'd been sober for seven months. Inspired by my sobriety, he chose to sober up too. We decided that I should move in with him to spend more time together when he was in town. We lived in a small room in a big loft in a worn-out, industrial building in Downtown LA, on the corner of South Santa Fe and 7th Street. We shared the space with a roommate.

It had thin walls, no ceiling and windows that didn't shut out the noise or the sunlight that flooded the loft when I got home early in the morning, ready to sleep. All the same, I liked Downtown LA; it felt like a concrete desert to me. Sometimes, I'd walk down a street and smell fresh paint from recently painted art murals or coffee wafting out of coffee shops. But what stood out to me the most was the LA River. It had been covered with concrete and yet one thin stream of water had managed to survive.

From time to time, I walked alone alongside what was left of the river flow, trying to picture how it was before—what sorts of trees and animals lived there. Then, I sat on the hot paved banks and imagined how hard that river had fought to stay alive.

That summer, Tyler and I traveled up the coast of California and spent a night in a cabin at Yosemite National Park. We got there at sunset. It was a clear night full of stars. We made sandwiches for dinner. There was a fresh breeze coming from the window we left open. I took a nice warm shower in the simple bathroom before bed. As I prepared to go to sleep, Tyler started screaming in rage. I froze. He gritted his teeth as he paced restlessly around our small room.

"I broke up with her because of you," he shouted at the top of his lungs. "What else do you want from me? You're now living in my room, *my* room, *my room!*" It had come from out of nowhere.

I sat watching helplessly. My body started going numb and his voice became distant. As my mind fled the scene, I could hear more and more of the animals outside. At some point, I asked him to close the window before someone called the police, and he stopped.

I felt cold. I needed to be hugged and protected and at that moment, he was my hugger and protector. I needed physical contact to squeeze away the shame that his screaming was my fault. I needed to maintain the illusion of what I thought love was, and to believe that the whole situation was perfectly normal for people in love.

As the fall approached, Tyler was ready to leave for Australia. I consciously decided to leave my job and my life behind to unconsciously start living his.

"You can help me with the merch and sell and control the inventory," he said as we prepared for the adventure.

I was going with him into the unknown of a new country I had never been to. In my years of drinking and using, moving around a lot was one of my strengths, but this time was different. I was only nine months sober and relearning how to live.

"I'm leaving with him, we've got it all planned," I said to Lisa before leaving. She was concerned and told me she was there for me whenever I needed her.

We arrived in Australia in early September 2015. The band was going on tour, and I was going to be Tyler's girlfriend and the merch girl. Three weeks into the tour, a couple of days before my birthday, the anniversary of my previous relapse, one of the band members got a call.

"What?" he said and asked the driver to stop the car.

The driver pulled onto the side of a road alongside a field of sunflowers, and the band member jumped out. We followed him.

He didn't seem to know how to deliver the news until he finally did: there had been a car accident on the way to the gig. The stage manager had been killed and the drummer was in a coma.

We were in shock and no one knew what to say, what to do or who to call. We just stood there for a while with no direction and a sense of overwhelming sadness. Our silence was broken only by a car passing us on the quiet road.

On the morning after the accident, back at the house we were staying at in Sydney, I met a version of Tyler that shook me.

"The show must go on, and this might bring us some publicity," Tyler said calmly, sitting on his computer. Then, like a lightning bolt, he stood up raging. He started screaming and throwing things around in the living room. Even though it wasn't the first time I had seen one of his episodes, I still stood there petrified, waiting for him to attack me. Instead, he stormed out and disappeared for hours.

The natural beauty of Australia helped keep me going. I spent hours at the white sand beaches swimming alone in the translucent water. The friendly cockatoos, those majestic white parrots with the yellow crests, made me feel so welcomed. The sleepy koala bears I spotted many times on the road and on tops of trees always made me smile, and the kangaroo families drinking water from wild ponds all reminded me that nature was an escape. I felt calm and peaceful there. It felt like love. It was a feeling Tyler was pushing me away from.

I turned one year sober in Australia on November 11, 2015. My friend, who I met during the tour in Sydney, took me to a meeting called The Rocks. The group gave me an amethyst and encouraged me to stay on the path. They knew that on tour, I would be exposed to all sorts of substances.

In the back of my mind, I kept telling myself that things would get better if only I cooked more, helped more, saved him more. I wanted to be the perfect girlfriend and have a partner that took care of me. No matter how much I tried, Tyler's intensity often escalated to insanity. I didn't like that, but I felt guilty about it. I thought it was my fault. So I kept trying to fix it.

We were back in Sydney for Christmas and one morning, I gathered the courage to finally ask him the question whose answer I was afraid of.

"Tyler, are you bipolar?"

"I am bipolar," he answered. "I can't control myself, and I can't treat it either or I'll lose my ability to play."

By New Year's Eve, I started letting go of control and came to accept I was powerless over the situation. We were back on the road, staying in a small town in the middle of nowhere for a concert. There was a heat wave and I was dehydrated, deflated and exhausted. As the night went on, I felt trapped at the venue with a bunch of drunks as I watched Tyler go back and forth to the bathroom to snort cocaine. He had relapsed, and I felt a cloud of darkness overwhelming me. I had to leave.

I found my way to the hotel, went to my room, got down on my knees and prayed. I didn't know what I was praying for or who I was praying to, but in my mind, I begged: *God, help me, please.* I fell into a deep sleep and when I woke up in the morning, the voice in my mind was loud and clear: *You've gotta get out. Just go.*

After a miserable New Year's, Tyler and I drove back to Sydney. One afternoon, I went to visit the Sydney Aquarium. I spent hours there watching the sharks with dead eyes swimming above my head, and in them, I saw myself dying again. I crossed the Sydney Bridge back and forth six times thinking, gaining the strength necessary to pack my things and move on. I was in the eye of the storm, but for some reason I was calm. Tyler was a ticking time bomb, ready to explode at any moment. I was a perfect target: vulnerable, alone and with nowhere to run.

My sponsor said, "Stay where the love is." To stay in Sydney was self-destruction; to leave was to return to myself and the support I needed. When I got back to the house, I had made my decision. I calmly asked Tyler to help me reschedule my flight back to Los Angeles the following day.

He was quiet for a moment and then said: "I know. It's been a lot. I'm sorry. And yes, I can help you." At the airport, I knew it was the last goodbye. He didn't. I didn't cry.

I got back to LA and despite my heavy heart, I just kept doing one right thing after the other. I sublet my friend's apartment. I realized I needed my family, so I traveled to Brazil. When Tyler called me, I was clear: "Tyler, we're done. I am breaking up with you. I wish you all the best."

As those words slid out of my mouth, I felt free, as if a heavy weight had been lifted from my body. I fell on the floor of my parents' living room and cried. Not because of Tyler, but for all the times I'd betrayed myself. My life flashed through my mind. I had lived away from love and kindness for too long. My heart was not meant to be an open wound, and I was not meant to feel like someone hard to love. I had fought to be here, and I was proud of the way I showed up for myself and for others.

It was a long walk back from Australia, and I finally understood that seeking in others what I so longed for myself was an impossible task I was no longer interested in achieving. My life was rich in experiences, and there were lessons in everything as long as I was open to learning them. The more vulnerable I was, the stronger I felt; the more I let go of control, the lighter I became.

I didn't have a perfect story, but I had survived, and it was time to embrace all that I was. Like the LA River had broken through the pavement, I broke through by choosing myself.

I WAS PLAYING SCRABBLE AND SUDDENLY, I KNEW I WAS GOING TO BE OKAY

NATALIE MARIE BROBIN

In February 2020, while I was 2,000 miles away from my home in Minnesota, my husband of almost 30 years asked for a divorce. It happened while he was visiting me in California, during my getaway from the Minnesota winters. We had had many discussions about how our life would work moving forward since I was in recovery from alcohol, and he still wanted a drinking lifestyle. Still, I couldn't believe our 30-year marriage was going to end because of alcohol.

I was in the middle of writing a book about my lack of self-care while raising our daughter, who had numerous health conditions. I had supported him and his work throughout our marriage; I even quit my job to become a stay-at-home mom. This was finally my chance to have a career in writing, and I felt I deserved his support.

I went home a month later and he continued to be as cold toward me as he had been for the previous two years. He also got drunk, which he had vowed never to do in front of me. I should have been finalizing my book, but I was completely overwhelmed by our living situation. So, three weeks after I got home, I said, "Okay, you can have your divorce."

I wasn't ready for the change, and I was completely devastated. My soon-to-be-ex (STBX) moved into the basement, and I lived upstairs with our young adult kids who were always coming and going. I asked my daughter, who had been planning to live at home until she started medical school in a few months, to move out because I knew my crying was only hurting her.

The shock and devastation came in waves, and the tears were endless. Like a river overflowing during a flood, I couldn't stop the tears. I just couldn't stop. I stopped eating and started losing weight quickly. I remember staring out the windows at the sky for hours at a time, not being able to get out of bed. I don't remember thinking of anything; I was in a suspended state where all I could do was lie there blankly. I had no thoughts or emotions. It was like I was dead inside.

I felt like I had been tossed aside. I'd spent the past 26 years raising our three kids, one of whom had a genetic disorder. I had thrown myself into my daughter's health issues and had become an expert within that community. My hard work had paid off because she was starting at medical school in the fall—and now he was divorcing me?

In eight months, all three of our kids would be college graduates. As a stay-at-home mom, I had been the constant in their lives. I had also given up a well-paid career after our third child was born and now it was too late to get back into it. He had retired the year before, and *now* he was divorcing me? I returned to those feelings of helplessness over and over again.

I had finally gotten to a good place after a nervous breakdown five years earlier in 2015, when my best friend died by suicide. The breakdown was complicated by childhood trauma and the real stresses of being a medical mom. Now, I was returning to those dark days. My PTSD symptoms returned.

I was having non-stop flashbacks to the shock I felt when my husband asked to divorce me. I felt spacey, like I was disconnected from my body. It was hard to focus on anything other than the grief. I had the worst physical pain all over my body, an achy, flu-like pain. I was chronically exhausted, no matter how much sleep I got at night, and I was crying constantly. It was agonizing.

I never thought our marriage would end the way it had. We had been drinking buddies almost our entire relationship; now that my relationship with alcohol was over, our marriage was apparently over, too.

My therapist and psychiatrist were worried about me, and so was I. They wanted me to return to inpatient trauma treatment. I managed to avoid that and saw my therapist more often instead.

Fortunately, I had recently joined a daily writing group. Turning my computer on each day at noon for a Zoom meeting gave my life focus and purpose. Knowing I was going to be on-screen helped slow down my tears. I tried to focus on writing. Most days, I just stared at the keys or wrote about my divorce instead of the book project I was supposed to be working on. Journaling my feelings was helping me process them; it was not dissimilar to talk therapy.

One particular passage I wrote was very telling of our marriage: "I have had to ask for affection for over two years. I've had to stand in front of my husband and ask for a hug in the morning and in the evening. This alienation of affection was because I told him that for my recovery, I couldn't be with someone who drank. It was life or death for me. He heard it as I was telling him what to do, and he never liked anyone telling him what to do."

This writing group became the cornerstone of my recovery from grief because it was a daily connection with a group of empathetic people. We supported each other through ups and downs, and I wasn't the only one going through a tough time. We bonded over shared stressors, but we also joked and laughed before our sessions started and after they ended. The world was in the middle of a pandemic, so visiting with friends was not possible. I missed seeing and hugging people, but now I had an online group to meet with day after day. I was comforted by the now-familiar faces on the screen. It made my grief more bearable.

Of course, I called my friends who had gone through divorces. Some of them were newly divorced and could still relate to my raw feelings, while others were further along in the process and could provide deeper insights. They let me talk and talk. I shared how I felt like I hadn't mattered at all. I cried about the loss of our family unit, and they listened. They understood me because they had gone through similar feelings of loss and despair.

It was helpful to know that crying every day for a year or more was normal and that all my feelings were valid. My friends were giving me the space I needed to grieve, and I started to lean into the tears. I knew I had to feel the pain to work through it. When my girlfriend had died, I numbed the pain with alcohol; this time, I was doing things differently.

Two months into our shared living arrangement, it was obvious my STBX could live in the basement indefinitely, and he said as much. I knew it was time to move on. I decided to move to Southern California to be near my oldest daughter. It was the first time I felt like I had some control over my life. When I told him I was moving out, I could tell he was shocked—this time, I was leaving him.

I was familiar with the area because I had spent the past two winters there, and my daughter picked out a mobile home for me to buy. It was a five-minute walk to the beach and affordable since it was a 55+ community, though I never thought I'd be happy to be over 55! It had been beautifully upgraded, so I didn't have to worry about major repairs or updating anything. I spent a couple of weeks there for my closing and my mood improved significantly. I was looking forward to learning to surf and scuba dive and to taking walks on the beach. I knew it would be a calm place for me to heal.

I still hadn't told many of my friends about the divorce and I knew it was time. My STBX told me he wasn't planning on telling anyone, and that I should wait until the moving van showed up. Of course, I couldn't be that cruel to the neighbors I had gotten to know over the past 29 years. I have always been a loyal and kind friend, and I knew I had to let them know I was leaving.

Neighbors and friends started asking about socially distanced get-togethers outside since the weather was warmer, and those invites were a catalyst for me to start breaking the news. Everyone was shocked and I didn't know what to say. I wasn't comfortable with it yet myself, so when people told me how shocked they were, I would just end up crying. Yes, my husband of 30 years was leaving me so he could continue to drink alcohol.

After a while, I posted about our divorce on Facebook:

Still reeling after my husband asked for a divorce four months ago. I made the hard decision to leave Minnesota for Oceanside, CA. I have not personally talked to many of you because it has just been too painful. I hope now that I've shared the news, it will be easier. I have been packing for six weeks and am still not done. Moving most of my stuff into storage. I plan to move in mid-September. Although Coley and Max are living their own lives, I will miss them terribly. And this beautiful home we designed and lovingly built 29 years ago will be hard to leave.

After that, people started calling me and I had walking dates almost daily until my move. I think I finally covered everyone when I sent out a holiday card with just me and my cat on it, as well as my new address. Looking back, I realized why it was so hard to tell people: because it made it real.

After I moved, I enjoyed decorating my 850-square-foot mobile home by myself—oh, the freedom! I took my time and put things wherever I wanted. I put pet steps all over the walls in my living room so my cat had lots of places to explore, which my STBX would not have let me do in the family home. He usually hated most things I bought for the house unless he was in on the decision. Once, I bought room dividers that ended up being very useful, but he always felt that they were unnecessary; then, during the divorce, he apparently changed his mind. He wanted to keep them! Ironic, right? For the first time in a long time, I had a space that was truly mine (and my cat's, of course).

On my daily visits to the beach, I started feeling whole again. At first, I just put my chair in the surf and stared at the waves; it was mesmerizing and comforting. After a while, I started walking along the beach and finding peace listening to the beach sounds, feeling the salty air on my cheeks and the sand on my toes. I also found solace in watching the sunsets. Every single one was so beautiful, like an amazing piece of artwork painted across the sky. I couldn't get enough. I had always felt peace in nature and had never lived so close to the ocean. It was the alone time that I had long been longing for.

After a couple of months, I started having some good days and making some friends. My neighbor at the mobile home park went to the beach every day as well, so I started getting to know her friends there. I also started meeting people within the park when they walked by or when I was on my way out for a walk. There was always someone to talk to. In our little community, we were all physically closer than we would've been in a regular neighborhood. It reminded me of summer camp—oh, how I loved going to camp!

As time passed and I had more and more good days, the pain of my separation still wouldn't leave me. My husband had served me with divorce papers right before I moved, and we were still hammering out details, so it wasn't legally over yet. Unfortunately, it's still not over. We are still negotiating how the money should be split, which is the saddest thing of all—possibly even sadder than losing 30 years of commitment to a bottle of wine.

About nine months after my STBX asked for a divorce, I was playing Scrabble with my daughter and her boyfriend. I realized that I hadn't enjoyed a Scrabble game in a long time. When I used to play with my STBX, he picked on me endlessly and ruined the fun of it. *From now on*, I thought, *I was going to enjoy games and enjoy my life.* At that moment, I suddenly knew with clarity what I hadn't known before: I was going to be okay. A few days later, the feeling hadn't passed—and so far, it still hasn't.

AFTER THE REIGN

KOREY POLLARD

The rain pounded in heavy, beautiful sheets on the half vinyl roof of my mother's gold 1972 Monte Carlo, its windshield wipers *fwipping* metronomically against the onslaught. It was peaceful, like being wrapped in a warm blanket fresh from the dryer, or the first time I smoked pot—before I discovered opiates and alcohol.

The acrid smoke of my mother's cigarette burned my eyes as usual. Why did my parents torture me and my sister by refusing to let us roll our windows down, all while holding their smoldering butts up to the driver's window's quarter-inch opening, essentially forcing all their secondhand smoke back in the car? It was as ridiculous as smoking sections on planes or in restaurants, which were just as commonplace in 1977.

"Father Abraham had seven sons; seven sons had Father Abraham. I am one of those, and so are you, so let's just praise the Lord!" My mother had a horrible singing voice, but she always claimed that God found it beautiful. My sister chimed right in without missing a beat—we were taught to obey, period.

Ordinarily, I would've complied, but not that day. I sat in silent defiance, tasting her secondhand smoke and coffee breath in my throat as the car heater blasted into my face from the vent in front of me, wishing I were anywhere but in that car.

"Why aren't you praising our Lord?" my mom asked.

"I don't want to! I hate these songs," I snarled.

My mother's faux spiritual composure drained from her face and she fell eerily silent, finally. For a moment I thought I had won, and the silence was golden. Immediately, I regretted my little insurrection.

An unsettling shadow deadened my mother's eyes as she pulled the car into a church parking lot, as far away from the building as possible—the fact it was not our church or destination was confusing. She smoked silently, gazing forward. The tension permeating the car was as palpable as the smoke stinging my eyes. Her silence eclipsed mine. *What was she doing?*

I sneaked another glance at my mother's face. The horror and betrayal in her eyes had me pinned to my seat, frozen like a deer in headlights. The silence I'd longed for was becoming more unsettling with every click of the cooling engine. The comforting sounds of the windshield wipers disappeared, displaced by my heart pounding in my ears.

She stubbed her cigarette in the ashtray, bolted from the driver's seat and crouched low, her face contorted with rage and chin nearly scraping the hood. Her fists pounded the hood in fury as she ran in the pouring rain to my side of the car. I had barely managed to lock the passenger side door a second before she grabbed the handle, shrieking, "Get out of the car *now!*" She paused, puzzled at my defiance before running ran back around to the driver's side.

I clambered across the seat and locked the driver's door. She hammered on the glass, water pouring from her nose and chin as she screamed. Her screeching scattered my little brain, dissolving my survival instincts like her spit in the rain. I was terrified.

My six-year-old sister was frozen in the back seat, eyes wide. I had backed us into a corner, and there was no escaping. The woman who was supposed to love and protect us was standing in the parking lot, shrieking unintelligibly, damning things like my rebellious heart at the top of her lungs. She was saying that God had demanded that she cleanse and break me.

And then, as quickly as the rage erupted, it was gone. The darkness left my mother's eyes. She coolly walked back to my door, mustering all the love and light she could to assure me that it was not me but the devil causing me to resist her and God's wishes. My mother's priorities always seemed to be in that order. It was all about her, followed by the desires she perceived were from God, the one she'd worked so hard to convince us would speak through her and on our behalf.

God shared with me that you should (fill in the blank with whatever *she* thought you should do or change).

As any trusting eight-year-old would, I eventually unlocked the door. Before my little fingers left the lock, the door was open and my mother's hand was locked onto my wrist and yanking me from the car, dragging me across the wet pavement to the front of the vehicle. I stared at the hubcap of our '72 Monte Carlo while my mother beat me with a stick she'd picked up somewhere in the parking lot.

She hit me repeatedly, from my shoulder blades to my calves. I lost track of time and all sensation left me: no pain, no shock or fear, only resignation. I must have deserved it.

My mother eventually came to her senses and pulled me to my feet. She hugged me as I burst into tears and informed me that she and God forgave me. She feigned an apology, but I did not believe her (even though I pretended to).

As we climbed back in the car, she started the engine, lit another cigarette, and drove in silence with the driver's window cracked. As the smoke burned my already salt-filled eyes, I remembered when my mother had caught me playing with matches in the backyard when I was five years old. To discourage me from playing with fire, she dragged me into the house, held me on her lap, lit three matches and blew them out one after the other, placing their smoldering, sulfurous heads on my tiny bare arm.

"See what happens when you play with matches?!" She screeched. "You get burned!"

As we pulled into the parking lot at the Bay Area School of Life, an Accelerated Christian Education school, it became clear my mother expected us to jump out of the car and act as if my impromptu beating hadn't happened. Combined with the memory and what she'd just done to me, it was the unexpressed expectation that I still act like a "good little boy" that severed the final strand of prepubescent trust I had for the woman who birthed me, and who claimed to be responsible for my well-being. It was as if a switch had flipped from on to off inside me; my soul went dark.

My sister bounced out and trotted into the building as expected, obedient and ever resilient. I came to know I was utterly alone at eight years old in an unsafe environment, and I kept to myself until I escaped at 17.

My mother and sister's adult relationship snowballed into a bizarrely enmeshed, 20-year-plus codependent traveling circus. It involved two cross-country relocations to small towns with no economies, a failed business, and oodles of mental, emotional, and spiritual oppression our mother called counseling (that expedited my sister's divorce and forced my sister and 24-year-old nephew to move in with my mother.)

Their living together culminated in my sister violently attacking our mother. My 24-year-old nephew, Chester Grant, witnessed the entire violent episode and was forced to restrain his mother. Finally, at 48 years old, my sister fled. She had suffered one too many verbal, spiritual, and emotional assaults and accusations of alleged drug abuse. My nephew had been isolated from the outside world with my mother and sister homeschooling him his entire life, as witness and victim to the bizarre accusations and manipulations of my mother's warped religious views.

He lived in holy terror that the "enemy," as my mother liked to call her interpretation of the devil, was prowling everywhere outside the bizarre sanctuary my mother believed her spirituality created, ready to consume him. He was told that if he did not obey, he could be kidnapped into child sex slavery or murdered at any time.

Chester had been compared to me over and over by my mother and sister.

"He's a mini-you!" my mother and sister would say.

This comparison with my nephew, whom I barely knew, stumped me for a myriad of reasons. How was he a mini-me? He was trapped. Chester never said no to Nana (which is what my mother wanted the grandkids to call her).

I had fought tooth and nail to get away from my mother and moved out of the house at 17, with the terror and shame of her weaponized religion still embedded in my soul and psyche. Chester, on the other hand, was still in her home paralyzed with fear, too anxious to leave her twisted reality.

With my sister missing and wandering the state homeless, I asked Chester if he wanted to leave Nana's house and live with me on several occasions, but the kid refused. He said he could not leave Nana and "auntie Katy," my mother's best friend who was also a part of the enmeshed 20-year traveling circus. Katy moved in with my mother after a divorce under the guise of being counseled by my mother. She rarely saw her own family; my mother told her over and over, "God has not released you to see them."

After Chester and I talked, I realized that although I ran from my painful childhood torments with drugs and alcohol and eventually replaced them with Hollywood, he and I were similar. I could not fathom the hold my mother had on him.

For nearly 30 years after I left that house, I, too, was driven by the need to please my mother and afraid to disagree with or disappoint her. She terrified, manipulated, and hurt me over the phone, through cards and letters and by using scripture, and I had no idea.

On August 31, 2020, a few months after my sister was released from jail and was undergoing medical treatment for her disorder, tragedy struck. The "enemy" my mother used to terrorize and manipulate us all about presented itself to my nephew on the face of my mother's best friend, Katy. The world will never know the things said and done to Chester Grant on all the days leading up to that day in August 2020. The only thing the world will ever know is that Chester grabbed my mother's gun and shot Katy in front of her. Eleven times.

When the call came from my father, I was barbecuing in my backyard, literally reflecting in awe and gratitude of how my life turned out with two amazing adult kids, a beautiful wife, an extended family, and a three-decade-long career in Hollywood as an assistant director.

My epiphany began on that call with my father. In an instant, so many things were different. Katy was dying, and Chester went from being isolated with his family to in jail and awaiting trial. My mother went from having control over my sister, her family, and Katy for decades to being utterly alone for the first time in her life.

Months after the horrific tragedy, Chester called me from jail and told me he had been diagnosed with schizophrenia, and that medication had changed everything for him. He also confided that the safest he had ever felt in his 24 years was when he'd been handcuffed and taken away from my mother, the unconscious architect of his childhood confusion and mental torment.

A little over a year before Chester's life-altering event, and with much help and immeasurable patience from my wife, I finally put a boundary between my mother and me.

Chester's experience helped me see that I, too, felt safest during my childhood when I walked into the chaos of a movie set for the first time at 12 years old, surrounded by more than

100 strangers for 12 hours a day for two weeks. At least I was away from my mother and her strange reality.

Thanks to Rob Reiner plucking me from obscurity and casting me as a barely-seen character in *Stand By Me* at 16, thus fanning the flames of my passion for movies, I found the bizarre courage to leave home two years later to join a different circus in Hollywood. I was lapsing in and out of alcoholism, addiction, abstinence, self-loathing, and debilitating anxiety for decades after leaving home (though I use the term "home" loosely).

I think of Chester often and am consumed with survivor's guilt. What could I have done for him? What can I do for him now? How did I make it out of my family without killing someone or taking my own life? How did I find sobriety, raise a family, grow professionally, and turn into a man who would set a boundary with my mother? I have no idea.

Slowly, by separating from my family of origin, learning to set personal boundaries and making many painful mistakes, a God beyond my comprehension, certainly not the one I was raised to believe in or beaten in the name of, introduced me to a confusing, unmerited, and life-altering grace, and infused me with love, forgiveness, hope, and courage. That I am now free of my mother's manipulation is still incomprehensible to me. But my mother's misguided beliefs have not stolen my love of the falling rain. I still cherish the feel and sound of the rain whenever I hear it or feel it.

I cannot comprehend how the pain in my life has driven me to a faith in God and proven over and over that nothing can separate me from the God of love and forgiveness—at least, when I remain open to lavishing that same grace upon others.

I am still struggling to forgive my mother, and I hope to find that strength one day. My heart aches at the thought of my nephew behind bars. I am learning to live in gratitude for unmerited grace, and to process the grief of my childhood and survivor's guilt after escaping the reign of my mother's mental illness.

THE FLOW OF SURRENDER

HEATHER LEVIN

As water steadily fills the lime green five-gallon bucket, I take the opportunity to grab the red broom and give the floor a quick sweep. The broom came with the house and the barn. It has seen better days, with its out-of-control wiry black bristles sprouting off in different directions, but it gets the job done. I imagine the broom looks the way I feel—confused, harried and utterly overwhelmed.

I guide the broom behind dried mud clumps, through the vertical hanging plastic strips meant to keep flies out, and along the track of the sliding inner barn door. As I push debris past a cache of sandbags, I remember shoveling the cold, flooded barn for two days last winter. I was alone while wheelbarrowing out puddles of muddied water, and those sandbags had helped control the flooding. I remember sobbing freely, physically exhausted and emotionally depleted.

It has been almost five years since our family started an animal sanctuary here, on our own five-acre property, and it hasn't always felt so lonely. We had started it together as a family, excited about our ideas for educational tours, a volunteer program, outreach, animal communication, and reiki sessions—and of course, with the goal of saving animals' lives.

Perhaps we rushed into it and should have taken it slower, done more research, and set up a solid infrastructure before taking in animals, or perhaps life was just going to happen no matter what we did. Whatever the reason, soon my husband was working out of state and no longer able to help. I struggled to find reliable, consistent volunteer support to help me with the animals, and because I was also parenting our two kids mostly alone, I found myself unable to handle all of the requirements to become a non-profit organization.

Everything shifted and at some point, we decided that we would no longer pursue opening our animal sanctuary to the public. We would still honor our commitment to the animals, but we would support them ourselves. The cows, pigs, chickens, and rabbits we rescued—and loved—would be just as much a part of our family as our dogs and cats inside the house.

Over the years, the kids became less involved with animal care and, as teenagers tend to do, focused on other interests. They helped out when they could, but the daily responsibilities, worry and stress fell on my shoulders. My husband was now traveling away from home for work every week. My 22-year marriage was ending, but that hadn't been a source of much emotional support anyway; there hadn't been nearly enough affection or space for me to express how overwhelmed I was.

We were determined to remain best friends and co-parent as best we could, and I believed I still had the strength to take care of the animals, the property, my family, and my blossoming career. The circumstances had changed, but I was not going to give up. The animals needed me, yes, but it was their unconditional love, pure kindness, and constant friendship that was a true gift to my soul. I liked to call the cows "land whales," due to their similarities: both large and slow-moving, but also wise, gentle, profoundly caring, and sensitive. All of the animals gave me the strength to keep going.

Still, every time a cow would limp or the pigs needed hoof trims, or a new mystery injury cropped up, I would stress and worry about whether or not I would be able to safely restrain them so that the vet could administer the care they needed. These were very large animals, and even though I was careful, I had already sustained a few lasting injuries. Large animal care had been a steep learning curve for me over the last few years; I grew up in Los Angeles, unfamiliar with this kind of lifestyle.

Even when all the animals were feeling fine, I was waiting for the other shoe to drop; it could all change in an instant. I would fill with anxiety at the thought that the cows would break the fences down and run away again, or that our 860-pound pig, Dolly, would once again get stuck in the pasture under a freezing night sky, injured and unable to move, and that I might have to handle other emergencies like those alone. I was consumed with worry, but I was always holding it all in, carrying the weight and living my life without reaching out for help.

I was an animal communicator and energy healer who was too emotionally stressed to help my own animals. In fact, I was neglecting my career. I was concerned about money, and because of my impending separation, I needed to start earning my own income. My disabled father's health was in rapid decline; I was his only child and I needed to figure out how to move him up to my house. Most importantly, I was concerned that I was increasingly missing out on time with my kids, meaningful time that I would never get back again.

On Thanksgiving (or "Thanksliving," as I like to call it, with an emphasis on keeping the turkey alive), I was faced with another pig emergency—a mystery eye injury—and the vet was unavailable. As my worry and feelings of helplessness continued to magnify, I remembered that I had recently found a broken raven feather. Inside the barn. This was not the first time, either. It had happened before, but the first one I'd seen had not been broken like this one. I took it as a sign; something big felt like it was moving closer, like a storm.

Our holiday meal was beautiful, but I couldn't eat. As we went around the table giving our thanks, I was filled with questions and preoccupied with thoughts of how to help our pig, myself, and all of us. My usual attitude of gratitude was lost in the depths of a darkness I struggled to escape. I wanted to cry, to dissolve, to disappear, because I couldn't see a way through it all. The emergencies, for both humans and non-humans, had been coming in relentless waves for months and, whether true or not, it felt like it all rested on my shoulders. I was breaking.

I needed help, but I wasn't sure what that would look like. Did I just need to hire someone? Or did I really need to hand everything over to someone else? Where would I find someone who would take such large animals and care for them for the rest of their lives? Cows can live up to 25 years, and usually, people don't try to keep them alive for that long. It seemed impossible to find a home for all of them, especially together, as a bonded group. Could my heart really handle saying goodbye to them?

As much as I loved them and considered them family, caring for so many animals felt like too much to handle. Our dream of starting an animal sanctuary was now ending after five years. It felt like a failure, and the weight of it felt debilitating. I didn't know the answers on that Thanksgiving, but I knew I needed to be open to possibilities. I realized I needed to surrender.

And so, on the morning after Thanksgiving, I called two friends who worked with rescued animals. Through my tears, I admitted I was in a dark place. I had never been so honest and vulnerable about my life before, as I'd been imprisoned by the belief that asking for help with a situation I had created was weak and shameful. I felt responsible for finding my own solution.

I had become so isolated by my fear and shame that I had forgotten that they understood what this life of caring for rescued animals was like. They listened, and their compassion and support uplifted me. As they showed me that day, the gift of kindness can shine a light in the darkest corners of the darkest moments.

One of my friends was the executive director for an animal

sanctuary nearby, one she had built from the ground up. She offered some great ideas that would keep the animals where they were by bringing in volunteers and sharing my property. It could become a second location for her sanctuary, offering a quarantine space for animals recovering from illness or surgery, or temporarily housing animals available for adoption. Her organization would then take over all the animal care. My animals would still be safe, cared for, and well-loved, but the responsibilities would now belong to her sanctuary staff and volunteers. I couldn't have imagined a better scenario; this was a win-win situation for all of us!

Over the next few days, the more we talked, the more ideas and possibilities we came up with that inspired us both. Our first plan was to clean and reorganize the barn, which the volunteers spent hours doing. When I saw it at the dinner time feeding, it was completely transformed. I was moved to tears; it looked absolutely incredible!

I felt supported, lighter. I started to see it all so differently.

My personal narrative shifted from one of failure and weakness to one of compassion and alignment. Overcome with gratitude, I laughed to myself at the seeming simplicity of it all. I had just needed to get out of my own way. When I emerged from my isolation and asked for help, I allowed myself to be woven into the fabric of a larger, shared vision. The result was that I had emerged with a renewed strength and a deeper ability to help others than I'd had before.

After surrendering, hope had flooded in.

Now, as I stand at the sink and water steadily fills the lime green five-gallon bucket, I savor the peace and quiet of the barn. The barn kitchen is especially cozy, and somehow the temperature is exactly what you need all year round—cool in the summer and warm in the winter, without any effort at all. As I wait for the buckets to fill, I take the time to be still and reflect.

This property has good bones and so much potential. As I run through the memories of the past five years like a filmstrip click-clacking through a projector, an extraordinary thought crosses my mind. This one has wings—big, beautiful wings that could carry me to the ends of the earth and back again. It's been through time and all the caverns of my soul, which is to say, it carries itself in wisdom. This thought was elegant and powerful, its impact immediate:

It takes more strength to let go than to hold on.

ABOUT THE CONTRIBUTORS

PETER AVILDSEN

Peter Avildsen is a writer, entrepreneur and somatic business consultant living in Los Angeles. He is writing a book of personal stories, cooking up a new product launch and completing the four-year training program at the Radical Aliveness Institute. You can find him at @avildsen on Twitter and Facebook and @peteravildsen (Instagram). Find out more about Peter at www.toolsandmethods.com.

NATALIE MARIE BROBIN

Natalie Marie Brobin has a BA in journalism and writes about parenting, trauma, loss and grief. A registered yoga instructor and a Yoga Recovery 2.0 Coach, Brobin's work has been published in The Mighty, Medium and Thrive Global. She has also been featured in multiple media outlets for her advocacy on behalf of Turner syndrome, the rare genetic disorder that affects her daughter. A dedicated volunteer for the Turner Syndrome Society of the United States, Brobin published her first book in March 2021 called *Everyday Self-Care and Your High-Needs Child.*

She recently moved to California and enjoys daily beach walks. Her blogs can be found at www.everydayself-care.com.

JEANNE FOOT

Jeanne Foot is the founder of The Recovery Concierge® (TRC), a boutique mental health and recovery services firm. Jeanne has been in recovery for 30 years and is a certified drug and alcohol counselor, a master trainer in clinical hypnotherapy and trained in somatic relational psychotherapy. Her customized concierge services support clients on their journey from "surviving to thriving" with a 97 percent success rate. As a transformational innovator, Jeanne developed the Total Recovery Practitioner™ Certification. Jeanne is the host of the Naturally High Podcast and has been featured in the Canadian Mental Health Journal, Elephant Journal, Thrive and Recovery Café. She is an original member of the Launch Pad Inner Circle. Find Jeanne on Instagram @the_recovery_concierge and @theholisticrecoveryspecialist, or on her website www.therecoveryconcierge.com.

TIMOTHY GAGER

Timothy Gager is the author of 16 books of fiction and poetry. His latest, *Poems of 2020*, is his ninth book of poetry. Timothy hosted the successful Dire Literary Series in Cambridge, Massachusetts from 2001 to 2018, and as a virtual series starting in 2020. Timothy was the co-founder of The Somerville News Writers Festival. He has had over one thousand works of fiction and poetry published, of which 16 have been nominated for the Pushcart Prize. His work has also been nominated for a Massachusetts Book Award, The Best of the Web, The Best Small Fictions anthology and has been read on National Public Radio.

BLAINE GRAY

Blaine was born and raised in Phoenix, Arizona and joined the Army at age 17. He served as a combat medic assigned to a reconnaissance platoon for the 2nd Battalion, 504th Parachute Infantry Regiment, 82nd Airborne Division, and was awarded a Combat Medical Badge and combat jump star for his participation in Operation Just Cause in Panama. These days, Blaine is a great father, an adequate husband and an actor. He is currently earning a degree in screenwriting at California State University, Northridge.

LISA HARRIS

Lisa is the author of two plays, *The Good Lover* (Producers Club, NYC) and *Circles* (Bootleg Theater, Los Angeles). Her first book will be published next year. In her past thespian life, Lisa was the original producer of the Obie Award-winning *Mabou Mines Dollhouse*, directed by Lee Breuer. Outside of work, Lisa is an active single mom of two teen sons and a passionate lover of the Seattle Seahawks. She serves on the board of Mental Health Advocacy Services (MHAS), a nonprofit organization protecting and advancing the legal rights of people with mental health disabilities.

JOHN FERREIRA

John Ferreira is a commercial airline pilot and flight instructor who discovered writing as a way to process the emotional turmoil he experienced around childhood neglect, addiction, and divorce. Using a pseudonym to start a personal blog (www. togetherwecanheal.com), John learned the importance of writing as a spectator, which has allowed him to observe his story rather than remain stuck in the chaos of the story itself. Through candid vulnerability and observation, John believes we can rise from our personal struggles by learning how to love and parent our inner children. John has been featured in Recovery Café and is an original member of the Launch Pad Inner Circle.

AMY LIZ HARRISON

Amy Liz Harrison is a native Californian and a Gen Xer. In her early years, she survived rotary phones, bad perms, and no seat belts in the rear-facing third seat of numerous family station wagons. In 2011, she found sobriety and joined a 12-step fellowship in which she remains active. Amy can be found meditating at the lake, clumsily practicing yoga, watching old MTV videos, and traveling to exotic lands (i.e., El Segundo). She lives with her Australian husband and their eight kids in Bellevue, Washington. Amy can also be found lurking on the internet at @amylizharrison on Instagram or at www.amylizharrison.com.

CHRIS JOSEPH

Chris Joseph is an odds-defying, stage-three pancreatic cancer survivor, as described in his 2020 book *Life is a Ride: My Unconventional Journey of Cancer Recovery*. Over the last 34 years, Chris Joseph has started and managed three environmental consulting businesses, launched two fan-funded music record companies and founded a non-profit charitable foundation. He has also dabbled in philanthropy, songwriting, and magazine writing. A native of Los Angeles, Chris has lived in Southern California all of his life. He has two teenage boys, a wonderful girlfriend and enjoys traveling, hiking, sports, music and connecting with other people.

JEFF KOBER

Jeff writes, teaches meditation and does tintype photography from his home in Studio City, California, which he shares with his wife, Adele Slaughter, their Labradoodle, Bud Powell, and their orange tabby cat, Pancho. Jeff wrote, acted in, and did tintype photography for *Lie Exposed*, a feature film starring Leslie Hope and Bruce Greenwood. His other acting credits include Debra Granik's *Leave No Trace* and Clint Eastwood's *Sully* as well as *Dead Sound, Beauty Mark, Lost Cat Corona, The Guilt Trip, The Walking Dead, Sons of Anarchy and many others.* His upcoming books include *The End of the Pain Factory: A Memoir* and *The Vedic World View 365.* Find Jeff on Instagram @jeffkobermeditation or online at www.jeff-kober.com.

BARBARA LEGERE

Barbara had a long career as an administrative assistant, though writing has always been her first love. As a single mom to her only child, she journeyed alongside her son through his mental health issues and addiction. She is writing a memoir about her son's suicide. Barbara is an advocate for harm reduction for addicts and an active member of various groups for parents of addicts and parents surviving the loss of children by suicide. She's a native of Southern California and lives with her sister, Therese, and her two dogs, cat and tortoise. Her hope is to keep her son's memory alive through her writing as a way of helping others who suffer from similar afflictions. Find her online at www.barbaralegere.com.

HEIDI LE

Heidi Le is a singer-songwriter and bestselling author of *Confessions of the Broken: A Codependent Rock Chick's Journey from Hopelessness to Healing.* She is working on her second book and passionately serves others through her Emotional Freedom Masterclass and as a life and recovery coach. Heidi and her husband, Ryan, live in the Santa Cruz Mountains with a cornucopia of rescue animals. Connect with Heidi at www.

heidilemusic.com or email her at info@heidilemusic.com if you connected with her story. She'd love to hear from you!

HEATHER LEVIN

Heather Levin is a writer, psychic medium, artist, and mother who lives in the Pacific Northwest among the trees and surrounded by the calls of foxes, quails, owls and ravens. Originally from Los Angeles, she has traveled extensively, but it is Siberia—specifically Lake Baikal—that has her heart. She loves animals, jazz, laughter and the Mid-Atlantic accent. She is thrilled to share her birthday with Oscar Wilde. She can be reached at www.heatherlevin.com or www.heatherlevinart.com.

SARA ONEIL

Sara ONeil is a casting director for reality television (NBC, Bravo, Playboy, WEtv, MTV, BET, VH1 and more) and some movies (*Death Link*, *Swipe Right*, *Wolf Mountain*) but moonlights as a spiritual junkie passionately studying spirituality, codependency, vibration and all things growth. Sara is a certified breathwork teacher and coach specializing in love and relationships. She is the author of the female empowerment book *There is a Woman* and co-author of the dating book *When the F Will He Text*. Connect with her at www.saraoneil.com.

SAMANTHA PERKINS

Samantha Perkins is the author of *Alive AF: One Anxious Mom's Journey to Becoming Alcohol Free*. Samantha is passionate about sharing the anxiety remedies and universal truths she has discovered about living without alcohol. She has always loved writing and chronicles her life on the blog Alive AF (Alcohol Free), which inspired her latest book. She is especially interested in uncovering the ubiquitous role alcohol plays in our everyday lives

—in everything from parenting, mental health, relationships and career choices. Samantha hosts wellness retreats, leads an online sober book club and helps women (especially mothers) rethink their relationship with alcohol.

KOREY POLLARD

Korey Pollard entered the entertainment industry living in the Pacific Northwest at twelve years old. At sixteen, a minor role in Rob Reiner's *Stand By Me* catapulted him into both the film industry and a cycle of addiction. Recovery helped him discover undiagnosed ADD and childhood traumas. He joined the Directors Guild of America in 1996, and makes a living as a first assistant director, though he has held numerous jobs in film and television production over three decades. As a writer, speaker, and adjunct instructor, he explores substance abuse, recovery, mental health and his creative journey in motion picture and television production. He is working on an upcoming memoir for film students and anyone enamored by Hollywood.

ERIN RANTA

Erin started writing as a way to share her story of recovery from alcohol and drugs. She grew up in Seattle, Washington, dancing ballet and modern dance, and received her Bachelor of Fine Arts in dance from Cornish College of the Arts. After dancing, she transitioned into teaching Pilates, which she has done for over 12 years in Seattle, Maui and now in New York City. During the pandemic, she partnered with Adrienne van der Valk to create REVA Recovery Support. REVA is a supplemental recovery program for women+ in most any phase of their sober journey who are looking to live the life they became sober for through holistic and somatic practices as well as embodiment and mindfulness work. Erin lives in New York City with her husband, daughter, and two dogs, Cherry and Fig.

BETH ROBINSON

Beth is a journalist, editor, ghostwriter, writing coach and visual artist. When not in her office, fingers poised thoughtfully over the keyboard while she looks out at the birds in her backyard for inspiration, she can be found snapping pictures on one of Michigan's beautiful trails (or online at www.brscribe.com).

SUELEN ROMANI

Suelen Romani is a photographer, filmmaker, actress, and licensed life coach. She is currently getting a bachelor's degree in journalism. She is a lover of culture and has had a lifetime interest in art, literature, music, movies, and theater. She has lived in many countries and explored their diversity, lifestyle, language, and cultural aspects outside conventional standards as a way to broaden her relationship with the world. Her work as a photographer has featured in galleries in London, Los Angeles, and São Paulo. As an actress, she worked in commercials and theater. This is her first publication in a book, and she is proud to be among such talented friends and writers. To get in touch with Suelen, find her on Instagram @suelenromani.cat or via her website www.suelenromani.com.

SUSAN ZINN

Susan Zinn, LPCC, LMHC, NCC, is a licensed psychotherapist, certified trauma and eating disorder specialist, and the founder of Westside Counseling Center in Santa Monica, California. Susan speaks nationally to academic, healthcare, government and business audiences on building strategies and environments that support mental wellness. She is an author, a mom to two teenagers, and the recipient of President Obama's Volunteer Service Award. Susan is a regular media contributor and can be found in the pages of *Forbes Magazine, The New York Post, Science*

Times, LA Parent Magazine and *Authority Magazine,* and has appeared as a guest host on iHeartRadio, BBC, talkRADIO and other media outlets. For more information about Susan, you can find her on Instagram at @SusanZinnTherapy or at www.susanzinntherapy.com.

CATHERINE JUST (COVER ARTIST)

Catherine Just is an artist, photographer and activist living in Los Angeles. Her work has appeared on the cover of *National Geographic*, inside *O Magazine* and in galleries internationally. She's the proud mama of her 12-year-old son, Max Harrison, who happens to have Down syndrome. She's developing the Max Harrison Foundation, whose first program will teach kids with Down syndrome how to use cameras for self-expression. Catherine leads artist retreats in France and teaches courses online using photography as a tool for transformation. Catherine mentors artists and entrepreneurs globally. Her work is available at https://www.catherinejust.com or on Instagram at @cjust.

CPSIA information can be obtained
at www.ICGtesting.com
Printed in the USA
FSHW020932201021